GW00384851

Book 3

THE HUNGER WINTER

**The Dutch in Wartime
Survivors Remember**

Edited by

Tom Bijvoet
&
Anne van Arragon Hutten

Mokeham Publishing Inc.

© 2013 Mokeham Publishing Inc.
PO Box 35026, Oakville, ON L6L 0C8, Canada
PO Box 559, Niagara Falls, NY 14304, USA
www.mokeham.com

Cover photograph by Rick Gleichmann

ISBN 978-0-9868308-9-1

Contents

On the front cover

'Woman on a Hunger Trek' is a monument to the women of Leeuwarden who made trips into the countryside in order to find food for their families and for fugitives hiding from the Nazis. The monument was the initiative of a fugitive staying with the Haanstra family, who kept him alive on the food gathered by the three Haanstra sisters on their many treks.

The monument was designed by Dutch sculptress Tineke Bot and unveiled on May 4, 1981, in the presence of the Haanstra sisters: A. van der Steeg-Haanstra, G. Stelpenstra-Haanstra and G. de Vries-Haanstra.

It is situated in the Prinsentuin (Princes Garden), a public park in Leeuwarden.

Introduction

Anne van Arragon Hutten

My parents had a child in each of 1938, 1940, 1941, 1942, 1944, and early 1945. Children needed to be fed, and even on a farm that could be difficult. Dad's crop of oats, the part that wasn't requisitioned, went to the local miller before being turned into porridge. There was no canned baby formula for me, five pounds at birth, nor Gerber's baby food when I was a few months older. My mother could not provide breast milk. I'm sure my diet in infancy was less than optimal, as it was for the siblings who followed.

Compared to city people, however, we had a great food supply. In the city money had lost all value in the later war years and food supplies went down drastically. In the second half of the war, what counted was whether you could wheedle and beg enough food out of farmers to survive for a few more days, or whether you had something of value to trade against a small bag of grain. It's a good thing the Dutch were used to grinding their own coffee beans, because their little hand-powered machines became essential for grinding that grain.

The women and teenagers who walked for days on end, pushing baby carriages or pulling rickety wagons just to get the most basic food for their family, were desperate. Many farmers opened their hearts and their storehouses, and doled out grain, milk, butter, one or two precious eggs, to the extent that they could.

My father had a small farm of about six acres. With all those young children he didn't have much to spare.

But he later told us a story that has stuck in my mind. It concerned his brother who lived in one of the western cities where people were literally starving to death.

One day a hongerlijder, literally translated as a 'hunger-sufferer', came to the door to ask for food. Dad was a sociable man and asked questions. Where are you from? Oh, I have a brother living there. Do you know such and such street, where he lives?

The upshot of it was that Dad gave the man a large piece of well-salted ham, from a pig that had probably been slaughtered illegally. The man was told that if he could deliver half of it to Dad's brother, Ben, he could keep the other half himself. It was not until many months after the war that Dad found out the man had kept his promise. Starving though he and his family were, he had acted honourably and taken half the precious meat to Dad's brother.

This true story forms a good antidote to those of the black market profiteers. During the war there were heroes and cowards, honorable men and despicable men, loyal citizens and traitors. For good reason, no one has contributed to this series a story of how their father made thousands of guilders by selling food to the starving at unreasonable prices. Read the stories, however, and you will see these forces at work. At any rate, the government's rejigging of the money supply after the war largely wiped out the gains of these war profiteers.

Reading the hunger stories raised a few questions in my mind. First, the Dutch aversion to eating potato peels was so well established that even during this period of starvation unto death, potatoes were still peeled and the peels were consumed only in utter desperation, diluted, if possible, with another vegetable. After the war, peelings were again relegated to hog feed.

Second, and more seriously, how was the traditionally male-headed hierarchy of the family affected after several years when fathers and older sons hid in attics and under the floor, or were absent in German work camps and prisons, while women and children did the hard work of gathering fuel and food? Not that the men had any choice, given the severe penalties attached to disobedience to the Nazi regime, but they must have lost some authority during that time. Is there any connection between this weakening of male power and the social chaos that erupted after the war was over?

The history of the Hunger Winter did not end with Liberation. It took many decades before all the long-term effects could be more fully measured. As one example, this dreadful period in Dutch history led to the finding that people who are conceived during times of hunger are at a higher risk for obesity, heart disease, and schizophrenia. One Dutch research team found that the time of conception is especially critical. Further studies are looking into the effects of hunger on a person's actual DNA, with some differences already found on one particular gene. The last war winter is now being described in scientific circles as 'the Dutch famine', since it was a very specific situation of which we know the cause, the beginning, and the end.

Although no doubt useful for such studies, Holland's Hunger Winter should never have happened. Given the German penchant for reprisals, the political reasons for calling a Dutch railroad strike were shortsighted. The

Nazis' complete intolerance for any kind of resistance against their reign of terror had been demonstrated time and again. At a time when listening to a radio broadcast could result in immediate banishment to German work camps, a broad-based action like a railway strike was guaranteed to result in calamity. Certainly food had already been scarce, due to its continuous forcible diversion to Germany, but the strike brought a complete and deliberate halt to any further food transports into the big cities.

After that, it was every man for himself. Concepts like respect for others' property, personal dignity, or honesty, largely collapsed. Sheer physical survival became the one driving force, as starving citizens tried to hang on until the inevitable liberation. For many thousands of them it would come too late.

Historical background

Tom Bijvoet

On June 6, 1944 the Allied forces invaded Normandy. After four long years of increasing terror and deprivation the Dutch people looked for a swift end to war and occupation. It was at least the general expectation that this would happen before the onset of winter, The successful campaign of the Allied forces, and the speed with which northern France and Belgium were taken, appeared to support this view.

When in early September the Allied advance seemed unstoppable, and people in the provinces of Limburg and Brabant could hear the sound of the big battle guns to the south, rumours started flying: liberation was imminent! In a fit of panic many Germans, and most collaborators, packed their bags and fled eastward. Tuesday September 5, 1944 became known in Holland as 'Crazy Tuesday'. People stood by the roadside waving the forbidden Dutch tricolour flag, jeering the fleeing enemy. Unfortunately it was logistically impossible for the Allied forces to sustain the speed of their campaign and, after they successfully took the strategic port of Antwerp in Belgium, the advance slowed down.

The Allies did continue to move ahead at a slower pace, however, and on September 12 American forces crossed the border into the southern part of Limburg where, on September 14, the first major city, Maastricht, was liberated.

To open up a corridor to IJssel Lake, and to isolate the German troops in the west of Holland, the Allies undertook Operation Market Garden. Its main objective was to gain control of the bridges across the wide rivers that divide the Netherlands into a northern and a southern part. Ultimately, the operation failed and the Allied advance was halted and contained by the Germans behind the natural barrier of the Rhine River and its tributaries.

On the day Operation Market Garden started, the Dutch government in exile in London called on the Dutch railway workers to go on strike in order to sabotage German operations. Thirty thousand railwaymen answered the call and went into hiding. The German authorities warned that a railway strike would hamper the transport of food supplies to the west of the country, and they made good on their threat by blocking all food shipments. This led to a famine that is remembered in The Netherlands as 'the Hunger Winter'.

All regular shipments of food, fuel and medicines stopped. Electricity and gas were cut off. Central kitchens supplied a watery soup made from potato peels, sugar beets or tulip bulbs. Rations dropped as low as 400 calories per day and those people who had any strength left travelled miles into the countryside to barter with farmers for food in exchange for items such as jewellery and bed linens.

To exacerbate this disastrous situation, the winter of 1944/45, although not one of the coldest on record, was extremely harsh. For fuel, people started cutting down trees and ripping out doors and window-casings from houses left abandoned by Jews who had been deported. Even the wooden blocks between the streetcar lines were collected and burned in makeshift stoves. The famine raged for up to six months. People collapsed and died in the streets. There was no wood for coffins, nor any capacity to bury the dead, who were simply piled up in makeshift morgues.

Churches and other organizations arranged for the evacuation of children to rural areas where food was more plentiful. Many children, staying in completely alien surroundings, did not see their parents for many months and could not be sure what they would find when they returned home.

In February some relief came when the Swedish Red Cross managed to persuade the Germans to allow them to send shipments of flour, which was then baked locally into white bread. Although its recipients passionately remember this bread, it had no significant nutritional value. More substantial were the supplies that Allied bombers dropped from the sky in April/May 1945 after reaching a deal with the occupying Germans.

By early May of 1945, when the western parts of The Netherlands were finally liberated, twenty to thirty thousand people had died of malnutrition and related causes. The after-effects of this famine would affect the health of many survivors for the rest of their lives.

Going to Friesland

Bill de Groot

Real hunger is something that occupies one's brain without room for anything else. My family lived in Bussum, North Holland. In the early days of World-War II, my father once said at the dinner table: "There will come a time when we will have no food to put on our plates." I was fourteen years old and will never forget his words.

Ever since the civil defense sirens had sounded in early May 1940 to tell us the German Wehrmacht had entered our country, life had changed dramatically. Hundreds of B-17 bombers of the 8th Air Force would fill the daylight skies with their silver bodies, on their way to Hitler's Germany. At night the R.A.F.'s Lancasters and Stirling bombers filled the sky with their droning, mixed with the sound of the German anti-aircraft guns, lit up by the waving beams of the searchlights. I remember a P-51 coming at our neighborhood with blazing guns, chasing and shooting down an Me-110. One bullet penetrated a clay tile roof, killing a girl playing the piano on the ground floor.

On February 17, 1945, my cousin and I, together with other children, were transported by horse drawn wagon to the harbor of Huizen on the IJssel Lake. There we transferred onto a large botter, an engine driven sailing ship built to carry freight. In order to avoid attention from the German or the Allied forces, the ship ran no lights. We quietly lay down in the ship's hold. Although the night was very dark, the captain certainly knew where he was going. We were packed in like sardines, as the boat was in fact too small to carry us all, It was my duty to empty the chamber pot when necessary, since I was closest to the hatch. Near Enkhuizen the ship stopped, as we could not enter the harbor of Workum before 8.00 a.m. I could see the harbor lights every time I emptied our pot.

We were glad when the boat started up again, but a fog came up and we ran aground outside Workum. After a long struggle we managed to get going again. Before we sailed on to Friesland we received buttered bread and meat. In Bolsward we were greeted by a pastor who accompanied us through the old town to his church, where we were served soup made with veal, from the soup kitchen in town. After that we rode on farm wagons to the town of Sneek. My cousin and I went to a building of the Red Cross, where we were allowed to stay for two nights. One of the female workers gave us a sandwich. I then started looking for transportation to Heerenveen. As it turned-out it was cattle market day in Sneek, and I noticed that there were boats from Heerenveen in the harbor. It rained, and we were lucky to find shelter in the cabin of a boat.

The following day I wanted to carry on to Wolvega, where we had a family friend who worked as housekeeper on a farm. We tried to hitchhike on the mail coach that ran between Heerenveen and Wolvega, but unfortunately it was full. We left Heerenveen on foot, but were lucky to get a ride with someone who was going to Oldeholtwolde, which was exactly where we wanted to go. After asking around for Marijke Terpstra, we finally met someone who told us where to find her. Marijke served us baked beans and bacon. We charged into the food but, having been hungry for so long, we almost passed out and had to go outside to vomit.

There were fifty milk cows on the farm, and calving had begun. There were also sixteen sheep and two horses. By March, the lambs were being born. I learned how to milk a cow.

A dreadful time

Adriana Heim

Rations at the local soup kitchen were getting smaller. On Wednesdays my sister and I had to go and get the food. Later in the morning we would eat the watery soup that had scraps of cabbage floating in it. After saying grace, the food was shared out and we would take grandmother's portion upstairs. Grandmother had suffered a stroke two years earlier and was bedridden. She and Dad, with his calm and constant faith, and we three girls were holding on to each other and growing closer during this dreadful time.

One day Dad was working on an old bicycle, trying to lay a heavy piece of rope around the wheels to serve as tires. "We need butter and milk", he explained, and told me where to go for it. He had drawn a map to the farm of someone he had met earlier and who was in need of a small bedroom mat. Bartering had become a way of life during the last years of the war since money had no value any more. Dad told me it would take about an hour to get to the farm.

Before I was halfway, the rope started to come off the wheels, so I took it all off and continued on. Riding on the metal rims was noisy, and I felt every bump in the road. However, I knew that it would have been much worse for Dad who was already in his fifties. I soon found the farmer and handed him the mat. With butter and milk in my bag I started the trip home. The dinner I made that evening tasted wonderfully delicious.

Potatoes in the skin

Afine Relk

Food was getting more and more scarce as the war went on. Eventually my mother did not have enough food to keep cooking for our boarders and she had to let them go, especially after she found one young man had been stealing dried peas from her bedroom where she had hidden them.

When the Germans closed off a street at both ends to go house to house looking for people who had gone into hiding, they also took anything else they wanted. Once a German went into our attic and filled his pockets with apples that Mom had saved for the winter.

During the last year of the war we ate potatoes with the skin still on. If you were lucky enough to get sugar beets you would grate them and boil them for syrup. The residue was mixed with flour, if you had any, and fried on the potbellied stove. I used to go to the farms on my bike to find milk. I once had two bottles of milk in my bag, when German soldiers stopped everybody. They took away my milk. I was eleven years old.

Once in a while there was horsemeat available at the butcher's. The doctor had given me a prescription because I was very anemic. My sister was so skinny that her ribs were showing, and had to go into hospital after the war because of suspected tuberculosis.

One of my Dutch farm friends here in Idaho told me that during the war his mother always had a big pot of soup on the go so that she could feed hungry folks. "That's all I can do for them," she had said.

A broken elbow

Anne Hendren

By November 1944, the weather became unbearably cold. Life was miserable in Utrecht. The only thing that had not been shut off was the water supply. There was little to no food, no warm clothing, no shoes, and no medication. The only way to obtain anything was by barter. But what did a dentist like my father have that he could use to barter with? Few of his patients were farmers. The prices for goods on the black market were astronomical. Unscrupulous people were becoming wealthy at the cost of their fellow countrymen. We called them war profiteers.

We wore our overcoats around the house, and filled hot water bottles on which to warm our hands and take to our bedrooms. I wore knitted socks in my father's army boots that entire winter, and considered myself lucky to have good shoes and warm feet.

The scarcity of food forced many people from the western part of Holland to trek to the eastern part, hoping to find wheat, meat, cabbage, potatoes, etc. Those farmers had never envisioned the wave of hungry people from Rotterdam, Amsterdam, The Hague, and Utrecht that came knocking on their doors. Since Leiden Road (Leidseweg), where we lived, was a main thoroughfare, some of those thousands of people stopped at our house for a rest, much needed medical care, or to use the bathroom. Many times Pap gave medical assistance to people with frozen hands or feet, horrible colds and fevers. A cup of warm surrogate tea was usually all that we could offer them.

Our own situation grew worse and one day it was decided that Hennie and I would cycle to friends living in Oudewater, about 25 miles from Utrecht, to see if we could get milk, cheese, eggs, or vegetables. We managed to get some food and got home again safely.

In February 1945, when I was sixteen years old, I teamed up with a girlfriend and her aunt in order to go east in search of food. My 14-year-old brother looked older than his age, and we feared that he could be picked up if he went too. We left Utrecht before daybreak, and joined a group of hungry people also heading east. We reached Harderwijk just before curfew. Suddenly we came to a German roadblock and all the men in our group were arrested. We were warned to turn back if we didn't want to run the risk of having our bikes confiscated. In total darkness we were guided to an empty school building where we found a place to sleep on a straw covered floor.

The Germans were cleverly using the long lines of hungry people as camouflage for their military transport. Therefore RAF planes often fired upon the columns. During such attacks we jumped in terror into the snow-filled ditches. Eventually we reached Zwolle, with its huge bridge over the IJssel River. Once across the bridge, we had another twenty miles to go to Ommen, where our friend, Ma Mooyboer lived.

We were so happy to have a bed to sleep in. As soon as we were rested we headed out to search for food. Ma knew the farmers and provided us with valuable information. My bike was soon loaded with forty pounds of grain, which I had bartered for two pairs of handmade ladies' shoes that had become too small for

Hennie and me. Within a half hour of leaving Ommen, the wooden tires on my bike skidded in the snow and I fell. My father's boots protected my ankles, but my right elbow took the full weight of the bicycle.

We found a doctor nearby and in his icy surgery he established that my elbow was broken and needed a cast. I could not return to Utrecht so I headed back to Ma's. My girlfriend and her aunt continued on to Utrecht, promising to let my parents know what had happened to me. I stayed with Ma for three weeks, after which I was able to join some people for the return trip to Utrecht. My parents were very relieved to see me again after four weeks. My father, medical man that he was, noticed my itchy skin and diagnosed scabies. A doctor's prescription for ointment and carbolic soap, a rare item, soon solved the problem.

We all used to go to bed ridiculously early out of sheer boredom. The extended periods of rest probably helped save our lives because being undernourished, poorly dressed and cold, bed rest was the best thing for us.

In March and April there were rumors that we were to be evacuated. The Allies were drawing nearer. My father built a cart to hold our valuables, with a seat for Mam to rest on. Our last few precious pieces of wood, and signs stolen from the Germans, were used to build the cart. It was massive and heavy, and hard to maneuver on its wooden wheels. Then we could not get it through the back gate to the street as Pap had not measured the width of the gate. This was one of our few comic moments during that last war year.

By the end of April, Hennie and I both had swollen thyroid glands and swollen joints in our hands and feet. Pap and Johan had big open sores on their legs.

Overnight shelter

Atie Lunshof Holmes

In that last war winter, when I was seventeen, I lived with my aunt and uncle in Utrecht because my parents were in the Dutch East Indies.

As my uncle knew several farmers in Harderwijk, we decided to go there to get some food. We took a sled and the first day we walked 14 miles to Amersfoort. A small hotel had a tiny room for us with two beds. We were surprised to find we had two roommates! I had to sleep with my uncle. But we were dead tired and thankful for a bed. The next day we reached Harderwijk. At the farm they fed us real country food. We were no longer used to that and our stomachs let us know it. We slept above the cows, and I had never seen a cow. At bedtime my legs wouldn't work and I had to be carried up.

The following day it was thawing, so we added wheels to our sled. After another night on the farm, with bacon pancakes for breakfast, we headed back to Utrecht. We didn't dare take the main road with our precious cargo, and whenever a car passed we hid our sled/wagon behind shrubbery. Besides, we were always afraid the Germans would pick up my uncle.

Close to Amersfoort a family let us sleep on a couple of chairs in their living room. We discovered that these people were Nazi sympathizers. When we left in the morning we did not feel well rested, and the last section of our trip seemed endless. We barely made it home before curfew where we were welcomed back as heroes, with our potatoes, butter, bacon, and sausage.

My dog had disappeared

Arie de Keyzer

I was fifteen, with two younger brothers. Our Rotterdam family suffered no real hunger. We lived near the Maas River and the Waal harbour, both clean bodies of water full of fish. Schools were closed and I went fishing, so we had fresh fish every day. In 1944 farmers were still growing a lot of grain and rapeseed, which unfortunately went to Germany. By the end of August, however, we started walking behind the mowing machine and in a few weeks had gleaned enough wheat and rye to make it through the winter. We also got rapeseed, for which my father manufactured a little oil press, and we made our own cooking oil.

During sugar beet harvest season, many trains loaded with beets crossed the city. Using a long, spiked stick we speared beets off the train cars. The juice was boiled down to syrup, and the pulp made into cookies. That same year, a coal depot area was cleaned out. The sand was full of coals, and we spent days up to our knees in icy running water collecting coals.

One of my uncles had a bakery. He sold little meringues, made of water, sweetener, colouring and baking powder. They managed to fill your stomach a little. He used a hand cranked whipping cream machine and I did the cranking for several weeks. After four hours, my arms gave out, and I was rewarded with half a loaf of unleavened bread, dense as wood.

In January, 1945, a friend and I headed for Drenthe, on bicycles with solid tires. We returned three weeks later with saddlebags full of food. Several weeks after that we went to the Achterhoek, the easternmost part of Gelderland. When I got back that time my dog had disappeared, almost certainly eaten by someone.

One grew up quickly

Audrey Hoeflok

My Dad was a night watchman at an office building in The Hague, which was occupied by German soldiers during the day. The Germans had stockpiled food in the basement and Dad and a colleague stole very small amounts at a time so the Germans would not get suspicious.

In early March of 1945 I set out to see a distant relative in the country in hopes of getting some food. My bike had small wooden blocks screwed into the wheel rims, with a strip of rubber from an old car tire nailed to them. It was not a smooth ride. After four hours of alternately riding and walking, I reached the farm and gave the farmer a letter from Dad and the money he had sent along. These people were very kind; they offered me a bacon sandwich and milk, and then stuffed my saddlebag with potatoes, onions, carrots, cabbage, flour, a small piece of bacon, three eggs, and a small bottle of cooking oil.

Back in The Hague I ran into a checkpoint, and a young German soldier poked around in my supplies. He was interested in the eggs but I pleaded with him to let me keep them for my sick mother. He said he wanted a date with me, so we agreed on a meeting place for the following day. Off I went with my treasures but minus my ID, which he kept. Of course I did not meet with him, but instead went to the police station to report that I had lost my ID. I was given a temporary one with the message to come back in one week to see if my ID had been turned in. It showed up after three weeks.

I was only sixteen then, but one grew up quickly in those days.

An embroidered tablecloth

Bep Crawford-Haagedoorn

I was born in Amsterdam and was twelve at the outbreak of war in 1940. It seemed the war went on and on, with curfews and blackouts, and having to tape up the windows. We never thought it would be five long years. Of course the last winter was the worst. No more wood to keep us warm as my dad had chopped up all the cupboard doors and other woodwork in the house. Nothing to eat but the potato peels that the Germans threw out after eating our nice Dutch potatoes, and of course there were the tulip bulbs, ugh.

My Mom and Dad had already bartered their gold rings, watches, and jewellery for food and potatoes. Later on we traded nice bedding and linens; the farmers would take no money. Mom had one nice large tablecloth that she had embroidered with lovely yellow roses and with lace all around. One day in the dark after curfew, my sister, Ans, and I took a big chance. We took the tablecloth, with mom's permission, and left the house on Ans' bike, which had no rubber tires but rope around the wheels. We rode to the nearest farm and exchanged the tablecloth for a small bag of potatoes - enough for one meal, but we were happy. Homeward again when all of a sudden we disappeared, bike and all, into a deep hole the Germans had dug. The bike was all right; we were a bit bruised, but I was still hanging on to the bag of potatoes. We were still able to have a good laugh, even with tears in our eyes. We were lucky we didn't meet any soldiers. Some things you just never forget.

We would not have made it

Bertine Strengholt

In early 1945 when I was 14, my mother and I headed north to see Father's relatives in the hope of getting some food. We lived half an hour east of Amsterdam. We joined hundreds of people on the same search for food. We were the fortunate ones, each having a bike with rubber tires. After two and a half days we reached our relatives and slept in a bed. We were given sausage, flour, a pound of butter, and a bottle of oil.

On the last day of our return trip we started our bicycle ride through the polders on a dirt road in pitch darkness. The road was a mess of slush, and our bikes, loaded now also with heavy loaves of dark rye bread that farmers had given us, kept sliding from under us. At one point my mother was so tired that she couldn't get up anymore.

As I was trying to get her up I saw a light coming towards us and a moment later a young man appeared. He helped my mother back up on the saddle and encouraged her to keep going. We followed him on the dark, slushy road until he looked at his watch and told us he had to get home before curfew. Being a young and able-bodied man, a labour camp would have been his immediate destiny if he were caught. We said goodbye and struggled on until finally the dirt road on the dike turned into a recognizable, paved street. When mother saw that, her last adrenaline kicked in and in another hour we were home. Without the young man's help we would never have made it.

Peat in the back yard

Cornelius Zaat

Shortly after Christmas of 1944, I was sitting close to our make-shift wood stove to get warm, when a kettle of water that was coming to a boil somehow tipped, dousing my left leg with hot, scalding water. Half of my lower leg was badly burned, and I was taken to the first aid nurse. The poor woman had the knowledge but not the equipment to treat me properly. I was laid up for well over two months with a large wound that kept on festering and took forever to heal. I still carry the large scar of this accident.

My brothers Nico, Aat and Gerry regularly drove their bikes with wooden tires, a little cart behind it, to North Holland to trade car batteries that had been fixed up by our older brother Peter, for bags of wheat, beans, potatoes or anything else edible. They were always afraid to lose their valuables at German checkpoints, either before of after the trades were made. Or worse, they could run into an unexpected raid and not only lose their valuables, but get deported to Germany.

Sometimes they stayed away for weeks, causing us great concern. And then, 'Glory be to God' they made it safely back home again.

Behind our house was a large pasture belonging to a dairy farmer. One day we noticed some men digging for peat. Peat is not a bad heating fuel when well dried. The men were cutting brick-shaped pieces and stacking them so the air would flow through. Dad asked them, "Do you think there might be peat in our back yard?"

The answer was, "I don't see why not." And, sure enough, when they were done in the backfield they started digging up our back yard and pretty soon piles of peat were stacked up behind our house, waiting for the wind and sun to dry them.

At some point there were telltale signs that the war might be coming to an end. First there were the beautiful loaves of white bread, donated by the Swedish Red Cross. They were distributed from a central location and people were accepting them with tears in their eyes. I also remember my dad suffering from hunger oedema, the pastor of our church coming to visit and giving Mom a pound of butter. What a generous gift that was! People in the cities would sell their house for a pound of butter.

Around the end of April, Allied planes started dropping food parcels on the still-occupied parts of Holland. The German authorities had given in to Allied demands that they be permitted to come to the aid of a starving nation.

Another victim

Dirk Hoogeveen

The winter of 1944/45 is generally remembered as an extremely cold one, but it's remembered so well because we had no fuel, and, with an empty stomach, everyone was cold and most uncomfortable.

Already by November 1944, many people had died of starvation. Even more people were dying after Christmas because the calorie content of food rations was being reduced at an ever increasing rate. In 1944 the allotted daily amount per person was 1600 calories. This was reduced to 900, then to 750, 600, 400, 250, and, finally, there was nothing left to eat.

Living in the country, we had no scarcity of food, and my mother never refused to give a meal to people who dropped by from the city. However, by the end of December there was nothing more to share. Food seekers, mostly women and children, continued coming to the countryside. After walking many miles in cold weather many collapsed, never to get up again. Others sat down by the side of the road and were later found to have died of hypothermia. It is estimated that more than 200,000 people suffered from severe malnutrition and an estimated 20,000 people died of starvation.

In January 1945 one of my sisters went on a food expedition to Friesland by bike, a return trip of about 220 miles. When she returned in February with some meat, she was ill and became bedridden with tuberculosis. After the war she died, another victim of the Hunger Winter.

Great respect

Doortje Shover

I was born on June 30, 1941. My family lived on the Boezem Singel in Rotterdam. The winter of 1944/45 was extremely cold. There was no food, no coal, and no electricity. People began going to the countryside to try and barter their cherished possessions for any type of food. My brave mother took the baby buggy (without a baby), walked to the German barracks, climbed over a fence and tried to steal their food.

Near us was a soup kitchen for children, where my sister and I had to go to get 'soup' which was nothing but some type of broth with one or two peas in it. However, we ate whatever we could find. My father and mother both suffered from hunger oedema because whatever food they could find they gave to us children. As there was no fuel whatsoever, people started secretly cutting down trees. Some also burned their cherished antiques in the coal stove.

People died of starvation in the streets. My father had heard about a man who sold potatoes but when he went there, the man charged 100 guilders for five pounds of potatoes. The black market was thriving and people parted with everything they had just to get some food.

Although the war was over on May 5, it continued to be the main topic of conversation at the dinner table for a long time afterwards. To this day I have a great respect for food. I will not throw food away. I cherish every meal I eat, and I am grateful to those brave Canadians and Americans who saved us from total starvation.

Home for Christmas

Ella Hoogwater

I was born in Hilversum in 1923.

In December, 1944, my sister and I, with our bicycles, managed to get a ride to Friesland on a garbage truck. We wanted to go to our aunt, my mother's sister, and collect some food. My father worked at the town hall, and that's how we were able to buy a permit for that ride. In Friesland we were given bacon, butter, and grain, which we put in our saddlebags. Then we biked home again.

At the end of the first day we were allowed to sleep in a farmer's barn in Wezep. The following day we had to contend with snow and ice on the road but we kept going and got home around five in the afternoon on Christmas Day.

Note: As of September 1944, the town of Hilversum organized food transports for its hard-pressed population. Among other methods of transportation, the town used garbage trucks, which had not been confiscated by the occupiers. The trucks were cleaned out and converted to run on methane gas before being put to work.

Sugar beets for my lunch

Else Bevelander

When Rotterdam was bombed, relatives of ours walked all the way to our house in The Hague. My mother welcomed them lovingly and gave them food and a place to sleep. They never returned to Rotterdam, as their house was gone.

At first we suffered no shortage of food or clothing, but that changed gradually. Food became ever more scarce, as the Nazis were transporting it all to Germany. We got our food from the gaarkeuken, the soup kitchen, where we could get a pan of soup. At first the portion was one liter, but soon it became half a liter, and then even less.

On January 1, 1945 a V2 rocket fell on Indigo Street, killing thirty-eight people. Deaths in The Hague rose to a level unheard of since 1870. Hunger oedema became common, especially among old people and children. During February and March 1945, an average of eighteen people died every day. On March 3, The Hague was hit by an Allied bombing raid that killed hundreds.

I worked at the public library, walking forty-five minutes morning and afternoon. For lunch, my mother packed me a paper bag with small pieces of sugar beets, which were quite filling. My boyfriend was hiding in the cellar of a bakeshop that was run by two sisters. One day German soldiers stepped into the shop and asked if they had any men hiding. The courageous women answered 'No', and gave the soldiers a loaf of bread.

Meat

Truus Leader

I lived in an orphanage in Amsterdam, because my parents could not cope. One day the cook told us that we were going to have meat. We were all very excited. She put a spoonful of tiny, grey pieces of meat on our plates. We all looked at it, wondering what kind of animal that was. There was talk of rats, of which there were plenty. People who had died in the streets from starvation, would have rats chewing on their bodies. I could not get myself to eat that meat after everybody was joking about what it was. We were told to hurry and eat quickly.

Slowly the others started leaving the dining room. I was all the way in the back, and stirred the pieces of meat around on my plate, hoping they would disappear. I tried swallowing a small piece without chewing. I gulped it down. "Hurry up Truus, you are not to leave until you have cleaned your plate," I was told.

It got dark outside and all the other girls had left the dining room. Later the lights were turned off. They did not realize I was still there. Finally I just gulped the last pieces down.

I ran to the dormitory where everybody was in bed already. I put on my nightgown. My stomach was churning and I felt sick. Suddenly, I sat up and emptied my stomach all over my nightgown and bed. The Sister in charge was called. She pulled me from the bed, pushed me into a dark broom closet in the hall, and locked the door. I was cold and stinky. Suddenly the air-raid sirens sounded. The children were all running to the exit. I screamed, but nobody heard me. Then the building became very quiet. There was no sound outside. Total silence. I hoped that the building would be bombed and that everybody would feel bad for forgetting me. I felt around me, and touched a wet mop. I tried cleaning my nightgown with it, but it just made me wetter. So there I sat on a cold floor in a dark closet. It might only have been half an hour, but to me it seemed much longer.

The all-clear siren sounded and everyone came back into the building. The same Sister opened the door and let me out. She hissed at me "Don't you tell anyone that I forgot you, you hear!"

Daily life in Amsterdam

Art Bos

I remember: Waiting in the lineup at a bakery to receive our weekly bread ration. Alongside, due to lack of power at the pumping stations, stinking sewage was overflowing the manholes in the road. Fortunately, there had been mass vaccinations against typhoid fever. Water rats, which normally stayed in the canals, now climbed the vertical brick walls of apartment blocks in search of food. There was no garbage around because whatever would burn was used for fuel. With no public transport and no usable bicycle, we walked to work. One sometimes saw a dog's head and skin in the gutter, people having eaten the dog, either their own or someone else's. Cats were long gone. Some people trapped birds on their apartment balcony for food. With no bicycle tires available, wooden sectional hoops with coil springs inside were used instead. They did not last. With no leather or rubber available, re-soling shoes was a problem. Linoleum floor covering worked fine as long as it did not get too wet. Tire sidewall worked best.

Those few who had a telephone could connect a very small bulb to the wires and have some light to read by, until the phones stopped working. Paperback pages had to do for toilet paper. Possessing a telephone directory was the ultimate luxury. Interesting colour combinations in knitted sweaters resulted from using woollen yarns salvaged from old sweaters. Looks were not important. The most common small talk? Joking about food, and how it used to taste!

They were nice to children

Icke (Freddi) Weston-Bousema

During the Hunger Winter, my father did not dare go outside, so my spunky mother would go out on her bicycle, with bags and bottles, to exchange anything of value for food. She would even beg for a cup of milk for her child at every farm she came to and pour it into the empty bottles she carried. Of course the milk was sour when she got home, but I got to drink it anyway. One time she came upon a fish hatchery and talked the owner into giving her a fish, a big carp. He knocked it on the head and put it in her bag.

We ate sugar beets, which my father, who could not cook at all, somehow managed to make into a cake. I, being a very picky eater, even during the war, would not touch this food. I remember once going to the soup kitchen with my mother, where they gave us some sort of porridge. I would not eat it. I never ate meat or fish before the war, after someone had told me the origin of meat. I always got the best of whatever my parents could scrounge up, despite my protestations.

The Germans billeted next door were nice to children, although I was not supposed to get near the place. One soldier gave me a piece of meat about the size of a dollar, but of course I did not eat meat so I ran home to give it to my father. To my surprise he was furious with me for taking anything from a German soldier and threw the meat in the garbage. This did not make very good sense to me.

Displaced persons

Frank VanderKley

In 1944 the food situation in The Hague had become intolerable. My mother had a cousin in the Wieringermeer polder near the Afsluitdijk in North Holland. This cousin had found a farmer and his wife, the Puttens, willing to take one of my brothers and me for the duration of the war. My brother Karel was five and I was nine.

Dad took us to the polder on his bike, Karel on a luggage carrier over the front wheel and me on the rear luggage carrier. It was about seventy miles. There were two tires on each wheel, one covering the holes in the other. Whenever Dad went back home from seeing us there, the bike carried a bushel of grain. Sometimes the Sicherheitsdienst would confiscate such loads. Dad, who was in the Resistance, still had the service revolver from when he was in the Dutch army. On one of the trips, when stopped by the confiscators, he pulled his revolver. He had those people jump, fully clothed, over the railing of the bridge. He didn't know what happened to them because he was in a hurry to get away from there.

We stayed on the farm for quite a while. The Puttens spoke Frisian and we had a hard time understanding them. We had lots to eat. We slept in the attic where we had a warm bed and a potty. We could not get down the ladder until the hatch was opened. The ladder and hatch were connected, so that when the ladder was pulled down from below, the hatch would open. If there ever had been a fire we would have had to break out through the roof tiles.

One of the barns was full of sheaves of grain that still had to be threshed. I helped by throwing sheaves down onto the threshing machine. There was a lot of vermin in the barn, and we killed weasels, mice, and rats with pitchforks. A lot of city people came down the road begging for food. The farmer's son and daughter and I scooped grain out of jute sacks and gave it to the people.

Our good luck did not last. Toward the end of the war the Germans decided to blow up the dykes around the polder. The water rushed in and flooded the land. The inundation was gradual, so we had time to flee. Whole families got onto carts pulled by one or two big Belgian workhorses, and made it to high ground. I met up with my mother, two brothers and one sister in a huge silo on the edge of the polder. We were now truly displaced persons.

I remember sitting near a sluice at the edge of the polder and noticing the water in the sluice get higher every time a ship went through. Looking over the land you could see bands of small animals such as rabbits, hares, weasels, and chickens trying to escape the encroaching water. After a few months sleeping in the huge silo, we were transported to a small village farther inland. We were housed in a farmhouse that was three or four hundred years old. The beds were built into the walls, with panels or shutters in front of them. They were filled with straw and the occasional mouse. My mother went almost berserk, as the accommodations were not to her liking. She made a fuss and we were moved to a bigger and richer farm near Spanbroek. We stayed there about a month. One day my mother was pumping water from a hand pump in the kitchen and a small frog came out into the glass from which she was about to drink. That sealed our stay there. The farmer's son took us in a landau, with a pregnant mare pulling it, to Alkmaar, where we had distant relatives. We did not last long there either because they had lots of children, very little food, and no room for more people.

We soon moved to a Red Cross center that turned out to be a hotbed of Dutch Resistance. It was a huge building and, roaming through it one day, I found a bathroom with in front of the window, hidden by a curtain, a machine gun that was trained on the German barracks across the street.

Food for Amsterdam

George Hansman

During the winter of 1944/45, my sister, who was eighteen, a girlfriend, and I, at sixteen, rented a handcart and joined the many people going north. We walked about fifty miles, sleeping in barns or stables. Sometimes farmers called us in and provided a hot meal, which was like heaven. One farmer's employee became very friendly with the girls and invited us into his house, telling us we could sleep on the floor on blankets he would provide. The girls, a little uneasy with his friendliness but looking forward to getting a good night's sleep in a warm house, decided that we should sleep in spoon formation. They did not trust the man and they were right. Fortunately we all woke up, which stopped anything from happening. The following morning, after a trip of about 70 miles, we arrived home with a bushel of potatoes, about sixty pounds of carrots, some grain, and flour.

A month later, my Dad and I made another trip but instead of a handcart we took his bike. We had some of my mother's clothing to trade and, if necessary, we could trade the bike too. We walked the bike all the way as we were not in good enough condition to ride it. On our way home, about ten miles from Amsterdam, we slept in a stable full of cows. We heard that Germans would be closing the roads into Amsterdam at five in the morning, to inspect or confiscate anything we carried. We left at 4.30 a.m. and arrived home with a few pounds of potatoes, carrots, and some rye.

Roelof is the shortest

Gertie Heinen

We lived in Bunschoten-Spakenburg, two fishing villages that had amalgamated. On June 8, 1944, my brother Roelof Adriaan was born. Around the same time Mom's sister, aunt Aartje, had a baby girl. She did not have enough milk to breastfeed the baby, and, this being the war, not enough cow milk was available either. So, three times a day aunt Aartje would come over with her daughter Stina, and Mom would nurse both babies. Having to share his mother's milk is probably why Roelof is the shortest of the brothers.

The winter that year was terrible for parts of Holland, especially for the cities. It was bitterly cold and food was extremely scarce. Many city dwellers would walk miles into the countryside as they searched for food. The situation was so dire that people resorted to eating tulip bulbs.

Our family had never been hungry as the fishermen could always provide fish, and the farmers provided farm products. Dad was very adept at knowing where and how to obtain the food we needed, and so provided well for us. He was also very generous to the hungry people from elsewhere who came to our town looking for food.

Trip to Overijssel

Note: Below are excerpts from a letter dated February 28, 1945 by 15-year-old Guus van der Weijden. Guus and three siblings were among a group of children from Amsterdam who were evacuated to Gramsbergen, Overijssel.

Dear father and mother,

In Amersfoort the driver stopped to fill up our wood stove again. One blanket got scorched, and a bag burst into flames. In Apeldoorn, friends of the driver were drummed out of bed to give us all a drink.

There were appalling numbers of vehicle wrecks lying by the roadside. In Deventer we crossed that beauty of a bridge across the IJssel River, among bombed and burned-out houses and piles of rubble. As the driver wanted to stop briefly, one of the front tires continued on its own. Truck trouble. We walked to Raalte. Around 3.30 a.m. we were taken to an evacuation shelter where we were given a place on straw in a corner. By 6.30 the stench drove us out of the place. At nine we were given three scoops of watery rye porridge, and a thin slice of bread and butter. We left on a farmer's cart.... At noon we got a cup of coffee in Lemelerberg, before Ommen, and Rev. Kunst sliced ten loaves of rye bread into chunks, maybe 1 inch square, and we each got two pieces. With the bumpy ride I developed a bad stomachache. I have a temporary place to stay in this town, and I can't tell you yet where I'm going next. Last night they gave me nine slices of buttered bread, one with sausage, one with cheese, and this morning two slices with syrup made from sugar beets, and a bacon pancake. Bye!

Guus.

Only one rijksdaalder

Hidde Yedema

In 1944 there was never enough food for me. Sometimes I thought Mem was trying to keep me from growing, and maybe she was successful because I never grew very tall. Mem sent us out to a farm to glean behind the wheat harvesters. My sisters and I came home with pillowcases full of wheat stalks and Mem showed us how to thresh them. On a windy day my brother and I took the grain to the dyke where we repeatedly poured the grain from one bucket into another. The wind blew the chaff away, and we were left with a nice layer of clean grain. We ground it in our coffee grinder and took the flour to the baker. It yielded one delicious loaf of bread.

One day I heard a rumour about wheat for sale on a farm. I raced home and told my mother. She gave me a pillowcase and a rijksdaalder (2.5 guilder coin), and said, "See how much you can get for that." I saw many other people walking in the same direction and guessed they were all going for wheat. I ran in the grass rather than on the pavement as it was faster that way, and passed as many people as I could. I met a man carrying a yoke from which hung two buckets. One held grain, the other milk. The man had a big smile on his face and I pictured him thinking of the bread he could make with that.

After crossing a small town I soon reached the road to the farm. Quickly passing yet one more person, I joined the lineup. A man showed us his bag of grain, saying it had only cost two rijksdaalders. I only had one, but calculated that it would still give me twice as much as what we had gained from the gleaning. I hoped the farmer would not run out by the time it was my turn. People were talking about the war, how long it would last, the battle at Arnhem, which baker was still in business, and where one could borrow a coffee grinder.

The farmer used a bucket to fill people's pillowcases, and everyone gave him money. Those must be the rijksdaalders, I guessed. I had mine in my hand, ready to tell him I could only afford half a bucket full.

The farmer didn't seem to see me, as he was talking to the man behind me. He filled his bucket again, took my pillowcase and dumped the whole bucketful into it. I yelled, "Whoa! I only have one rijksdaalder, I can only buy half a bucketful."

The farmer walked to the barn, found a piece of string, and tied up the pillowcase. "Turn around!" he said and tied the pillowcase to my body. He then tousled my hair and said, "That's how we treat boys with only one rijksdaalder. Make sure you get home safely!"

I don't believe my feet touched the ground all the way home.

A fearful time

Riekje Brandsma

As there were no dairy farmers in our village, I had to go to a neighbouring village to fetch milk. I rode my bike in all kinds of weather, carrying the milk in glass bottles wrapped in old clothes. On Saturday mornings I had to go for groceries for which we had ration coupons. An old man in the back of the grocery store took your coupons and gave you a list of what you could buy. You had to bring your own jars if you needed oil, syrup or jam

It was a fearful time. We heard stories of people who had been sent to prison camp because they had slaughtered a pig or sheep for their own use, without permission. Still, we were well off compared to the people in the big cities.

My favourite doll

Jantina Smittenaar

I remember being cold and hungry, especially during the last year of the war. We got 'soup' from a soup kitchen. It was more grey water than soup. We went to farmers and traded for food. We traded my very favourite doll with all her clothes, and an antique doll carriage for five pounds of split peas.

Whenever I am in Holland now and have a chance to go to a rummage sale I look for one of those dolls. I would still buy it, although I know that I am too old to play with dolls.

Household help was needed

Janna de Klerk

I was 10 years old and living on a farm just outside Amsterdam when the war broke out. The Germans took one of our two horses in 1940 and stole the other one in 1943. We really needed those horses, as our potato field was ten minutes away. So, Dad would load the wagon while my brother and I were now the horses holding up the two wagon poles. Dad, Mom, and my sister pushed the wagon. A neighbour farmer and his two sons watched us but did not offer to help even though they had two horses in their barn. Another farmer asked dad to come and work for him, for which he got 4 pints of milk plus some wheat every week. Mom baked bread from that.

Dad became very ill but we still collected the milk and wheat. However, after a while the farmer said to my brother, "I heard your father is going to die; I have to hire another man. So don't come back here anymore for food." Now we were in big trouble. Mom made bread from sugar beets. One day the Germans came, and stomped all over our vegetable garden. A interpreter told Dad, "You'd better get everything out of your garden because tomorrow we are going to make trenches here, and all your trees will be topped." That night we went to bed with a stomachache.

One day my sister and brother came home with two slices of bread each. They told me where they had gotten it and I should go there. I thought 'never!' Mom gave me the slice that was meant for her. That Saturday night I prayed before going to sleep, "O Lord, do something!" Sunday morning in church our pastor announced: "There is a boat leaving for Groningen tomorrow. If you want your children on that boat be there early, it will take from babies till fourteen-year-olds." I said: "Thank you Lord".

On our way to the boat the next morning, we saw a man pushing a wheelbarrow with a dead person in it. There was not even wood for coffins anymore. At the pier there was a lineup. Mothers handed their babies to a nurse who put them in a basket that was then lowered down into the ship.

Two little girls, Mary and Nelly, about five and seven years old stood next to me. They were very skinny. When a nurse told the captain that they could not take any more children down below as it was packed, he said he could not send those kids home again. He opened a door to a room with a table in the middle and benches all around, and told us to go in. A nurse asked me how old I was and when I told her fourteen, she said I was in charge. Some kids had brought a pillow and soon lay down on the floor. One of the boys said. "We are going to a land where there is plenty to eat." Mary and Nelly settled on the bench next to me and put their head on my lap. Mary said, "Will you take care of us, you are our cousin, okay? Now tell us a story."

A nurse brought in a pail of grey potato peel soup. One small boy said, "Don't eat yet, we have to pray." He and his younger brother went down on their knees and prayed the Lord's Prayer. I had a lump in my throat. In the morning a nurse woke me and told me to follow her. Mary and her sister came too. We boarded one of several buses, the three of us sharing one bench. Then the babies were brought in. We each got one and a baby bottle. Soon we were all little mothers feeding babies. Mary said her baby was sound asleep. I knew at once that the baby was dead and called the nurse. She held my shoulder for a moment and looked at me; I was in tears.

When we arrived in the city of Groningen, the babies were taken to a medical centre, and then we went to a church. Somehow the other kids had found me and we stayed together. I overheard nurses talking about a contagious disease that had spread among some children, and that no one was to go in or out. We were just in the church hall, so I took the kids outside with me. When another group of kids arrived by bus, I told them not to go in, and we just sat there on our suitcases. A nurse told us not to let anyone enter, and later a sign appeared on the door.

People from other churches came to collect us and one after another the kids were picked up. I stayed one night with the woman who got me. The following day we went to Grootegast, where we were loaded onto a horse-drawn wagon and taken into the country. A boy walked me to a windmill where three ladies in local costume were waiting. They talked in their local dialect, but I could understand them. They said I was too small. It is true that I was small for my age. The boy then took me home to his place where there was already another girl from our group, Bep. The lady there served us baked potatoes with a salad, delicious. She asked if I could darn stockings. Bep and I started to darn underwear and stockings. When the father came home, he told me they wanted a girl because his wife had been in hospital for a long time and needed help with the housework. Bep told him I was there to be fed and regain my strength, but I said I had no problem with helping out. He said I could stay. Bep said to me, "Are you blind? People who put you to work after fifteen minutes in their house. You're in for something!"

A couple of weeks later Bep was laid up in bed with tuberculosis.

Rabbit food

Jacoba Bessey

By September 1944, food was getting scarce. Schools helped out by serving some kind of vegetable mush to the students. The vegetables were cooked in big kettles that looked like garbage cans, and my five-year-old sister, Martha, wouldn't eat because the food came out of a garbage can. Dad did what he could. He biked from farm to farm to find food. Mom used to worry when he was away because the Germans were still taking all men between eighteen and forty to work in German factories. Dad was born in 1905, which made him thirty-nine years old. We found out later that he had changed his birth year on his ID card from 1905 to 1903, which made him two years older.

Once he brought home a bag of apples. We ate many of them and paid dearly for it. I got a really bad case of diarrhea and was hallucinating. Mom thought she was going to lose me, but a neighbour had some tablets that helped me get better. My dad and an uncle came home one day with a sheep. They had stolen it from a farm that the Germans kept for their own use. Mom was worried sick that someone would find out, but Dad figured that with our six kids and my uncle's five kids, we needed food. They butchered it in our bathroom and divided the meat. What I remember is trying to clean up all the blood and grease with no soap or hot water.

Besides working for the Resistance, my sister Johanna also worked in a music store. Her boss hoarded potatoes under the shelves where he kept musical instruments, and, when the boss wasn't in, I would go in with a couple of shopping bags and swipe some potatoes. It wasn't much but at least it would give us a few meals. Sometimes Johanna managed to buy a small loaf of bread on the black market for twenty-five guilders.

German soldiers loved their music and would come into the store looking for records. Johanna refused to go out with them but would accept food in exchange for records. Once a Nazi soldier brought in a big ham covered in oil and grease. The Allies had bombed their food storage and the ham was all he had been able to save. He got his records and we washed the ham and had a meal made in heaven. I was thirteen at the time and needed all the nourishment I could get.

Our neighbour had a rabbit named Hans. My sister Ann decided that Hans would make a better meal than a pet so she stuffed him inside her jacket and brought him home. Some time later the neighbour came over, all upset because her little Hans was missing. Ann volunteered to scour the neighbourhood with her to look for the rabbit, while knowing exactly where little Hans was. Apart from that we had little or no meat. Everybody was in the same boat. We heard of people just dropping dead in the street. They were so weak they didn't have the will to go on living.

A dangerous town

Jenny Blad

I was three years old when the war broke out. My dad went to Germany of his own free will, believing that he could do more for his family that way. My dad loved the German people and they loved him, but not the Nazis. Dad was able to send money home while other people who were forced to work for the German Nazis were not able to do this. It was up to my mom now to take care of my sister Greetje and me. Living in the north of Holland, the first few years were not too bad for us, but that slowly changed. Mother had to sell her best linen, gold watch, and sewing machine for food. The farmers did not care for money as it was worth nothing. A bottle of oil would sell for 250 guilders. My mother would bring home dried fish that stank something awful. We had to eat it anyway.

We would chew tar and turned it into chewing gum. You could do the same with grain. We kids would go to where the grain was being loaded onto trains, and we would pick up what had fallen on the ground. It takes a long time to chew that grain but believe me, it will turn into gum.

We may have been kids but we did things that were beyond our age. We would jump onto trucks loaded with sugar beets, and throw them off the truck so people could make sugar. I remember one day when I was sent shopping for groceries at the corner store. From the store I could see the school that was occupied by the Germans. I also saw a truck heaped high with coal, but no Germans in sight, so I climbed onto that truck and started to shovel the coal down. What was amazing was how quickly people realized what was going on. They came with buckets to scoop up what they could. When others took over from me to shovel more coal down, I ran home to tell my mother to go and get some for us too. The Germans let us be for a while; they must have known what was going on. Most of them were mere boys.

We were also sustained by the soup kitchen. One day a neighbor called to say that there was meat in the soup that day. Quickly I was sent to get some of that good stuff. In the meantime, our neighbor had found the source of the meat: it was the tail of a mouse. I can't remember if we ate that soup.

Food was so scarce that mother decided to leave the city and go to her sister's who lived in the country, closer to the farmers. She loaded up a pushcart with some of our belongings, and then found a boat that would take us to my aunt's place, some twelve miles away from our city, in a town called Appingedam. When we arrived there, we found my aunt in bed with tuberculosis. We were there only a few weeks when the Germans ordered everyone to leave town. We were once again on the move. Where to now? We eventually came to a farm where a good farmer and his wife lived. They allowed the sick, including my aunt, to move into the farmhouse. The others had to go to the barn and sleep in the hay. There were quite a few of us, all making a place for ourselves as best we could. It was not easy sleeping with all those strangers; their noises used to keep me awake for a long time. Several of the men, including my uncle, helped the farmer milk his cows. We were allowed to drink the milk. As much as I love milk, I sure had to get used to drinking milk still warm from the cow.

To feed the family, mother and my uncle, and sometimes others, would walk back to town and collect all the food they could carry. People built fireplaces from bricks so they could cook. I only remember eating pancakes there.

It was dangerous going back to town, as the Germans were shooting at the Canadian soldiers who were in Holland liberating the Dutch. From where we were staying, we could see that the town was burning. But my mother and several other brave souls still went back day after day. If they found no food in one house, they would go into another. In those days it was not considered looting or stealing, merely survival.

One day, mother went back to town with one of the men from the farm. When she was ready to go back to the farm she called out to the man, who was standing in the doorway. At that moment a shell hit him, and he was killed instantly. Time and again people went back; what else could they do? You had to go, if you wanted to eat and take care of your family.

Always talking about food

Johanna Van Breda-Csank

Stores were empty, no food, no soap, absolutely nothing, only a lot of fleas. It is impossible for people to understand if they have not lived through it.

In the streets of Holland, people were dying. I wondered where all the cats and dogs had gone until I saw some 'furry coats' lying in the gutter. I worried about our own dog.

I stood in line for hours for a little soup that looked like black mud. I could see the lice crawling on the coats of the people standing in line in front of me. When the guy ladling out the soup spilled some of it, men fell on their knees licking it off the dirty street.

My sister and I lay in bed thinking about food, always talking about food. One day my cousin came over and told me there was a train going up north with girls who worked for Gazan, a garment factory in The Hague. "I know the foreman", she said. "If you want to go, be at the station at eight tonight." This was my way out. I was at the station that evening but my cousin did not show up. I could not go home, since nobody was allowed to be out after eight. There was a group of girls on board. We only traveled by night. The train stopped once in a while; they let us out when nature called. We just went any place, in the dark.

When we got to our destination there were very good people who filled our hungry bellies. Not long after that the Canadians freed us.

I never should have done it

Jerry Meents

My father was in hiding in our apartment in August 1944, when my sister Jetje was born. After giving birth my mother could not do anything. At fourteen, I was the oldest of the children and had to do something to keep our family of nine alive. Food rations were down to 450 calories a day. We ate tulip bulbs, sugar beets, dogs, cats, anything to fill our stomachs. I became a thief. I stole money, bread, ration cards, anything I could trade or sell for food. One night I went to rob a bakery and came home with thirteen loaves of bread. We ate them all in one evening. In another robbery I swiped half a case of potato starch that was normally used for starching clothes. When it was cooked in water, without salt or flavouring, it tasted horrible but it took the pain of hunger away for a while.

If we had something that needed to be cooked, we used a stove made from a vegetable can. Because there was no coal we used all the doors in the house for fuel. We also took all the wood we could find out of apartments belonging to Jews who had been deported.

In December I stole a flashlight from a man who worked in one of the soup kitchens. It was a knijpkat flashlight, one you had to keep squeezing to get light. This man had sold us some spoiled pea soup and I was going to get even. I sold the flashlight for about 150 guilders, with which I bought food on the black market. This gave us something to eat on New Year's Eve.

The following day I was arrested and put in jail at the

police station in Linnaeus Street. I shared a cell with a man who had killed someone for stealing his bicycle that didn't even have tires. The man told me what to say or not say to the police. Because of his instructions the police could not prove that I had stolen the flashlight and they had to let me go.

I also stole a cat from a friend of my mother's, but then I was unable to kill it. A neighbour, who wanted the cat's skin to put in his shoes, killed it and we ate the cat. Even though it was a big cat, there was not much for each of us. However, it tasted very good, even without salt. I never told the cat's owner the truth, though I am sure she suspected me.

In February I stole somebody's wallet. It had enough money in it to buy a piece of meat for us. The man was selling merchandise on the black market and was not hungry like we were. I never should have done it, though, as he was well acquainted with my parents and had even given my mother some food once.

Pitchforks

John Eyking

My father was a market gardener. We grew tulips, daffodils and hyacinths but as we could no longer export, we began to grow vegetables, grain, and fruit instead.

By the last winter of the war the southern provinces of The Netherlands had been liberated but those north of the rivers were still occupied. To protect our animals we put them all together in large barns and took turns guarding them. We used pitchforks for weapons. People were hungry, and stealing to survive. Every day, groups of people from Amsterdam would come by our farm, begging, or offering their possessions in exchange for food, sometimes asking for just one potato. Unscrupulous farmers would trade the clothes off people's backs for food; it was terrible. The city people would pass us again on their way back to Amsterdam.

I remember being scared, sitting in our cellar during air raids. Mother used holy water to protect us. Along our coast everyone, except essential people such as farmers, was forced to move inland. The coastal lands were cleared of trees, leaving nothing but four-foot stumps as a deterrent to tanks. The Germans built bunkers or fortresses every 500 yards, with walls and canals. One night, when the German general in charge was expected to be passing through the main street in Beverwijk, the Resistance placed a bomb in the middle of the street. It blew up a military vehicle, but not the one carrying the general. Within one hour, ten men in the area were dragged out of their homes and shot in retaliation. Fortunately for us, we lived almost a mile away and did not witness this slaughter.

In the morning of May 4, big Super Ford planes flew overhead, dropping food parcels. One carrier must have had some left over and dropped a load by our farm. There were parcels everywhere. Father kept some of the food for us. After Liberation we partied!

Eight legs of lamb

John Keulen

As the war dragged on it was becoming difficult to feed the young men who were in hiding with us. As they did not officially exist, they were not eligible for ration cards. In addition, there was an influx of so-called 'hunger children' from big cities such as Amsterdam and Rotterdam where people were starving.

These children came to rural Friesland by the thousands, together with adult escorts. Families in small villages were asked to take in these malnourished children and provide for them. Many families with children of their own took in one or sometimes two. Our family took in Charlie, an eleven-year-old boy from Amsterdam. It was obvious he was an undisciplined child but it didn't take my mother long to make him toe the line. He turned into a well-behaved boy, and before long spoke Frisian as well.

Much more food was needed now to feed all the kids, plus all the young men in hiding. Ration cards were issued through the county courthouse to registered citizens only, and were kept under lock and key. The Resistance decided to do night raids on various courthouses in order to obtain ration coupons. They used the same methods the Germans used with their razzias, that is, surround the courthouse and gain forcible entry by brandishing weapons. Their success rate was high, as most of the time courthouses were not guarded at night. The Resistance then distributed the ration cards where they were most needed.

The Resistance obtained their weapons from British planes that dropped them during the night. Most of the weapons were Sten guns, cheap, automatic short-barreled rifles entirely made of metal but effective at close range. Some of the weapon drops went sour as the Germans got wind of them by decoding radio messages. It was a very dangerous occupation and many Resistance members paid with their lives when things went wrong. Still there was not enough food to feed all the needy children. The dairy factories started communal kitchens. The food was distributed at noon from strategic points in town. There was no meat in this hot, cooked food, but plenty of mashed potatoes and vegetables. My brother or I collected it in a bucket.

Charlie's appetite knew no bounds. (As an aside, he returned to his single mother in Amsterdam, where my brother George and I visited him by train in 1946. Charlie must have been about fourteen then, and a high-strung city kid. It was our first trip away from home, and we were in awe of the streetcars and all the hustle and bustle of a big city. We were less impressed with Charlie's behaviour. He had returned to his old ways. His mother treated us with kindness, however. She probably felt she had to protect these country bumpkins from Friesland.)

To get meat on the table, Father thought it would be a good idea to butcher some sheep. This was illegal, of course, as all available meat, especially beef, was destined for Germany. Although accurate records had to be kept of all farm animals, sheep fell into a gray area. It was possible to report fewer newborn lambs than the actual number. This enabled the farmers to barter a lamb or two for tobacco, coffee or tea. An active black market ensued, in which a good portion of the population engaged.

My father managed to find a partner who was familiar with butchering, and he asked him to find some lambs. Our cellar, the coolest place in the house, became a slaughterhouse. Father's partner became adept at cutting the sheep's throat and butchering the carcass in the confined space. Initially our family was not fond of mutton but we adapted to the taste. As there was more meat than we could eat, Dad distributed it through clandestine channels. His partner got half to distribute as he wished.

Then my father got caught, just as he left the house with thirty pounds of neatly packaged meat. He was not sixty feet from home when two armed Landwachters, Dutch traitors who worked as inspectors for the Germans, confronted him. These men were more feared and despised than the Germans themselves. They ordered my father to stop but he shot into the greengrocer's shop in a futile attempt to escape. They were right behind him, and it didn't take them long to find the heart of the operation. They found eight legs of lamb and Father's partner, Hendrik, who was still cleaning up. Both men were arrested and taken to the old federal prison in Leeuwarden. Most of the prisoners were members of the Resistance and served as hostages, or were awaiting transport to labour or concentration camps. Mother was very much afraid that Father might crack under brutal questioning and that his Resistance activities in connection with downed pilots would come to light. But Father divulged nothing and, after four days, was set free. Earlier, Dad had become friendly with a

German named Hans, who was the commanding officer of the local German force. My dad used to supply him with tobacco that he grew in the attic. I have a strong suspicion that Hans and his German colleagues were interested in seeing my father freed so that their tobacco source would not dry up.

You pick it up!

Karel Stuut

I was 12 years old in 1944 and living in Haarlem. It was the Hunger Winter. My father was in good physical condition and, together with a colleague, biked to Overijssel and Gelderland to find food for our family of four. Since bicycle tires were not available, rubber garden hoses held together with steel wire functioned as tires. They took along bed sheets and towels from our linen cupboard to barter for food.

My father came back with a bushel of wheat on the back of his bicycle. On his return trip my father was stopped in Amersfoort by an officer of the Waffen SS who asked him what was in the jute bag. My father told him that it was wheat to bake bread. The German officer told my father that he was going to confiscate the bag. My father took a sharp knife out of his pocket and ripped the bag apart, saying, "Here it is, you will have to pick it up from the ground." The German officer was so perplexed that he let the two men go. The wheat was still on the ground.

My father was a supervisor for the installation of central heating systems in public and private buildings. The Germans had taken possession of several large homes in Haarlem and my father's company got the contract to install central heating systems in a couple of these villas. My father made sure that the work was progressing very, very slowly for two reasons. One, he did not want to provide comfortable quarters for the Germans, and two, he was able to steal food from their kitchens. I clearly remember him coming home one day riding a bakfiets, a carrier bike, on which was a large crate of tools. At the very bottom of the crate was a wooden delivery box from a well-known pastry shop with twenty-four pastries in it, stolen from the Germans. We had not had any pastries for a very long time.

I found out
how a beggar feels

Karl Vandegoede

My family lived just outside the city of Utrecht. In September 1944 things started to go from bad to worse. The Germans took all our food and even with ration coupons you often could not get what you needed.

I was then fifteen years old and could still move around freely. Once you turned sixteen you could be picked up and sent to Germany. I spent a lot of time going from farm to farm trying to find something to eat. When it got colder it became harder to get around. But I had no choice. I did my utmost to keep the family alive. Every day I went to collect sticks and pieces of wood from a park close by. I could carry just enough to cook one pot of food on the wood stove.

When it was harvest time a farmer gave me permission to collect ears of wheat after the field had been harvested. It took more than one day to fill a bag. At home I rubbed the ears between my fingers to remove the kernels. Then I had to blow the chaff away and finally ended up with a small bag of wheat which I ground into flour in the coffee grinder that was attached to the inside of the cellar door. I took the flour to the bakery next door so that they could bake a loaf of bread with it. One loaf was far from enough for a family of seven, but every little bit helps.

The only way to get food was to trade something that

the farmers needed. It so happened that we had lots of bleach. The farmers needed bleach and I built up a route where, on a more or less regular basis, I would trade a bottle of bleach for two liters of milk.

The milk was not homogenized and always needed to be boiled before use. But before it was boiled it was put in the cellar in a wide container so that the following morning we could skim the cream off the top. This was then put in a wide-necked bottle and after doing this several times there would be enough cream in the bottle to make butter. We took turns shaking the bottle until the butter appeared. That took a long time. But we had butter.

Together with a friend, I went to the eastern part of the country, which was mainly agricultural. Our bikes were very old but we went more than sixty miles on the first day. One was always in danger on the road. The only vehicles on the road belonged to the German army and if Allied planes spotted them they would pelt them with machine gun fire. We had to cross a bridge over a big river. Bridges were also often targets for air attacks.

At night we slept in a stable on straw between the cows. All night long we heard the cows moaning and dropping their poop in the gutter behind them, and us. The next morning we went out trying to collect food. It took three days before we had enough. When we got hungry we would knock on doors asking for something to eat. Then I found out how a beggar feels.

Each night we went back to the same place to sleep. By that time it was usually dark. The Germans had a place close by, from where they fired their V2 rockets to England. The noise scared the daylights out of us. Those rockets had not been perfected yet and some of them would go up only so far and then fall to the ground somewhere. One night, while pushing our bikes back to where we were going to sleep, we heard the sound of a rocket suddenly stop, which meant that it would come down and explode. That could be anywhere, maybe too close for comfort. I still remember the feeling I had while walking in the dark in an unknown area not knowing where the rocket would fall. That was a scary experience. We felt better after we had heard the explosion.

At last we were on our way back home. If anything, going home was even scarier than going out. People who had collected food often were stopped on their way home by the German police and had their food taken away from them. However, we made it home safely. With what we brought, and our daily pea soup from the soup kitchen, we could survive a little longer.

I realized what it meant to be hungry

Maria Neijmeijer

We were living on a farm just south of Amsterdam. During the Hunger Winter we filled bottles with milk for people from Amsterdam at eighteen cents per liter. After I had filled the bottles for one lady, she rang the doorbell again and asked if she would be allowed to pick up the dried beans she saw in the gravel. My Dad had been forced by the Germans to grow beans during the summer of 1944. While storing them on the upper floor of the coach house, some of the beans had fallen onto the gravel. This lady asked for permission to pick them up, and when I said, "Oh yes", she asked for a paper bag. She was on all fours for a long time and in the end she maybe had a pound and a half of beans. I watched her and realized what it meant to be hungry. Because I lived on the farm I was never hungry, but oh, I will never forget this lady.

Nor will I forget when the airplanes came and I saw the food parcels come down. We received a parcel with white bread, pork and beans, sugar, gum, and other goods. There were strawberries in the garden and Mom put strawberries on the white bread, and that tasted better than any cake I ever had.

At the end of the war we had prisoners of war at our farm, who were very hungry. One morning we woke up to the bleating of lambs in our meadow. The soldiers had slaughtered some sheep to have something to eat.

There were so many of them

Kees Vermeer

During the last four months of the occupation, our supply of food and other commodities dwindled considerably. Once or twice a week I went for food to the Soup kitchen. The soup and mashed potatoes we got contained beets, carrots and turnips and a little meat. The meat had a lot of fat, cartilage, hairy skin and bones. We once found a mouse in the soup but on the whole, the food was not bad. My sisters, my brother Jan and I ate everything but not the mouse. My parents were fussy. After seeing the food from the soup kitchen, they did not eat any of it. We teased our mother about having some 'very delicious burnt lumpy porridge'.

I liked going to the Soup kitchen, as it was always entertaining. People standing in line for the food, which was discharged from large barrels, joked about their contents and the pails they carried. Ordinary pails had become scarce and many came with slop pails or bedpans. One time there was an air raid while we stood in line. Everybody dove for cover behind garden walls and buildings, while pails flew noisily all over the place. It took some time to sort them out.

Even when conditions grew worse, we never starved. We kept warm by cutting down trees and digging out willow stumps for heating. The stumps were from fields reserved by farmers for growing willows. Digging and cutting out roots was hard work. We carried the roots home on a sleigh. Burning these stumps in our stove

71

provided little heat and much smoke, but it was better than nothing. Occasionally, on skates, we ran down coots hampered by ice frozen to their feet. They were a welcome treat at the dinner table. Jan, by approaching upwind, once surprised a hare at the point of bursting out of its burrow, by jumping on top of it. Catching the hare was made possible by the presence of a heavy icy snow crust over the burrow. The hare had had a hard time breaking through the crust, which helped Jan spot the animal before it could get away. That hare became a feast for our family.

We felt extremely sorry for the people in the big cities. People walked all the way from Rotterdam to our region and traded any valuables they possessed for a sack of potatoes. Sometimes there were long lines of people pushing handcarts on the road to Rotterdam. They looked terribly tired with their hollow cheeks, worn out clothes, and shoes through which their toes protruded. I pitied them and sometimes helped to push their carts for a long way while they limped along. But how much help can one give? There were so many of them.

He could not eat it

Lisette de Groot

On December 1, 1944, while my mother was giving birth to my brother, there was a knock on the door. My father threw caution to the wind and opened the door himself. Two German soldiers walked in and wanted to go upstairs. My father explained that his wife was upstairs and in labour, but the soldiers pushed him aside and ran upstairs, entering the room next to my mother's. In that room stood a burning candle, its light shining through a small opening in the curtains. This was a violation of blackout regulations. The soldiers quickly drew the curtains, warned that it should not happen again, and left. My father was much relieved because the Germans could easily have taken him away.

We ate sugar beets daily. Also fodder beets, which were a little less sweet. Eel traps that yielded big, fat eels were set out in the creek that ran through our yard. It was my father's duty to kill and skin them. They would slither over the patio with their heads up, making a 'kah-kah' sound. Dad, who was very sensitive and hated this job, would grab an eel to chop its head off. The eel would wriggle its whole body around Dad's arm. Finally, the eels where chopped into five-inch pieces and fried in a pan with a lid, because those pieces were still wriggling and jumping. The meat tasted delicious. It was very greasy but we all had a need for fat.

There was one other occasion when we had meat. This time my Dad shot a big, fat wood pigeon out of a blue spruce with his air gun. He was surprised at his own skill. Dad plucked the bird, Mom cooked it, but when we sat down to dinner Dad could not bring himself to even have a taste.

We did not drink the milk

Maria Blöte Rademaker

Cutting down trees was not permitted, but my father woke me at 5 a.m. after he had seen a stump one day. We sawed and sawed. When we were halfway through, a policeman came by. He confiscated the saw and told us to get lost. In the afternoon Dad went to the police station to retrieve his saw. He told the bewildered cop that he wasn't bothering anyone and couldn't let his family freeze to death.

Dad and a neighbour walked all the way from Amsterdam to Den Helder pushing a handcart. They gathered up beans, peas, and potatoes. On the return trip they were invited by a farm couple in Limmen to have supper and stay the night. That was amazing. In the morning after they had breakfast, more goods were loaded onto their cart, and these wonderful people offered to help them again next time.

My sister Truus and I, twelve and eleven years old respectively, were sent the next time. We walked from Amsterdam to Limmen, about twenty miles, and arrived late in the evening. We were fed, our cart was filled, and we were put to bed. Not quite halfway home the next day, our cart broke an axle. We decided that one of us would push and the other, bending double, would try to keep the cart balanced, so that none of our precious food would be lost. That was very hard, and we had to go such a long distance. Suddenly a truck stopped beside us. The driver felt so sorry for us, he offered us a lift as far as Zaandam. From there we walked another three hours until we got home, completely worn out. But we were happy not to have lost any food, and we had not even drunk any of the milk!

Mice in a trap

Michael van der Boon

As soon as it was dark, the streets came alive with shadowy figures, sneaking around with their hand-powered flashlights, called knijpkat, squeeze-cat. We could hear them purring past our house as people hunted for food, wood, or coal. After burning all their own doors and stair banisters, people started chopping down trees and carting away fences from around parks and homes. They even dug out the tree stumps. Pigs and cows were stolen and slaughtered right on the spot. Few people worried about whether stealing was bad.

One night my dad was asked to slaughter a pig for someone. He had received part of the pig as his wages and carted it home on a sled covered by a lot of blankets. At one point he was stopped by a well-meaning person who told him that there was blood dripping from the sled and that it was making a trail in the snow. Even though my dad was a butcher by trade, having illegally slaughtered meat was a serious offense. Besides, he had escaped from forced labour. He made sure no more blood showed after that.

One day while we were in an air raid shelter, a horse standing in front of a cart was killed. When we came out of the shelter, we saw people swarming the horse, attacking it with knives and saws, more ferocious than lions attacking a wildebeest. In very short order there was nothing left of the horse but bones.

No cat was safe. They appeared on restaurant menus

as 'rabbit'. Soon there weren't any cats around. Dogs were kept inside to save them from meeting the same fate.

On the way to and from school I saw people dying in the streets. People were often too weak themselves to help a fallen person and so they would just leave them there. A boy from my class, Dirk, was standing on the sidewalk in front of the school one morning watching us play. His much-too-big clothes were hanging from his skinny shoulders. Suddenly he turned, stumbled and lay down, curling up on the cold brick. I ran over to cover him with my jacket while other children ran for help. It was a long wait and, cradling the boy, I told him not to be afraid, even though I was terrified myself. Realizing what was about to happen, I said, "I'm right here with you." The boy's lips trembled and a faint smile appeared. Then he didn't seem to hear any more and his body went limp. He was covered with a blanket and carried off. I remember shaking uncontrollably. I can still see that tiny body under the blanket.

Defying the Germans, roadblocks and Allied air raids, thousands of city people, including my mother, swarmed the countryside, begging farmers for food or just taking anything they could find. My mother always seemed to return with something: a few eggs wrapped up in lots of paper so they wouldn't break, or some potatoes, even some milk one time. She told us how she would walk back with her bicycle in hand, cotton shopping bags hanging from the handlebars, sometimes 20 or 25 miles. She would refuse to sit down and rest, probably because she knew that once she sat down, she might not get up again. She would crawl through the fields, bicycle and all, hiding behind bushes, sleeping in an empty barn, anything to make it home to us somehow without being detected, or the Nazis might have confiscated everything.

The tulip bulbs we had, after removing the bitter cores, were either boiled or fried. We were warned against eating hyacinth bulbs, which were poisonous and would cause violent stomach cramps. People by now were eating anything: dog food, sawdust scraped from the butcher's block, candles. People had swollen faces, wounds that would not heal, and legs that were bloated from hunger. Deaths happened so fast that the bodies had to be laid in churches as well as mortuaries. When a Jewish person who had been in hiding for several years died, the body would be carried out at night and simply shoved into a murky canal.

We were not the only ones who were famished. Mice and rats were coming into the house, looking for food. My mother had set up a trap one day and the following morning there were two mice in it that had attacked the bait simultaneously. The trap had not been able to close completely and the mice were still alive. We stared at the creatures on the floor. They looked up at us with their beady eyes and started to struggle again.

"Look at these poor devils", my mother said." They're just like us, mice in a trap, half dead, and still struggling to be free."

Somehow we made it through, and five months later, after having lost everything in a bombing raid, we were liberated. In our two western provinces some 20,000 people had died from starvation.

Her husband's body

Robert Colyn

Note: Robert Colyn spent the war in Haarlem while his parents were in the Dutch East Indies. Tiek Heinsius was the girl he would later marry.

By the beginning of 1945, the western provinces suffered extreme food and fuel shortages.

To get food, Tiek and her sisters volunteered to bike across Holland to Heerde, a small rural town in the eastern part of the country, where they had friends. Traveling on their rickety bikes, the girls risked hazardous conditions on the road, such as rape by German soldiers, and strafing from Allied planes, not to speak of mere exhaustion. Riding a bicycle without inflated tires would have been tiring for a healthy, muscular man, let alone for these malnourished Heinsius girls. Tiek made the 75-mile trip to Heerde twice that winter, spending the night in a vacant industrial building, together with other travelers looking for food. To prevent their precious food from being stolen, the girls had to sleep clutching their bags.

They encountered many other destitute people. Some, particularly the elderly, succumbed under the strain, or simply froze to death. I personally observed an old woman who was returning to Amsterdam. The very senior, totally exhausted and dazed woman was pushing a handcart that contained a sack of potatoes along with the frozen body of her husband. She shuffled past me with others, in the direction of Schiphol airport.

One ladle of tulip bulb soup

John van der Meer

I was 14 years old at the time of the Hunger Winter, and if the Canadian Army had not liberated us on May 5, 1945, I would not be here to tell this story.

Towards the beginning of fall we could not get food or much of anything else with the ration coupons we had. Stoves and heaters could not be used because they took too much fuel. Instead we made a small stove out of a coffee tin.

By Christmas things became very bad. We had to line up at a cart in the street that dispensed one ladle of tulip bulb soup per person per day. Even the half loaf of bread per person per week that we had received earlier was now no longer available. Electricity had been cut off.

One day a boy of about sixteen approached me and asked me to join the Resistance movement. I was interested, but when he started to teach me how to shoot a gun I got cold feet. It was a good thing I refused, for within a few weeks the Gestapo found the group and, according to his neighbours, the boy was shot while running away. If he had not died right there, who knows, he might have given me away too. I never told my parents about this, of course.

Around the same time we heard that a store near our house, where only Germans were allowed to shop, had been overrun by a crowd, because they had baking oil in stock. We used that to burn an oil lamp at night. I went there, but it was all over by the time I got there. A passing German patrol car had arrived before I had and had randomly taken eight people hostage. They had to line up in front of the store and were shot. No one was allowed to remove the bodies, which were left outside the store as a warning. Not long thereafter a cart full of potatoes, which I had followed, parked in front of a German office. People crowded around it and I joined them. The two men in charge of the cart started throwing out the potatoes and I made my getaway with a good portion of them tucked under my shirt. The crowd had been very threatening to the two men. On my way home I saw a German patrol car speeding up to the cart but once again I got away in time.

With two other boys I went to the park to cut down a tree for firewood. As we were cutting it up, a German patrol arrived. The Germans were friendly and told us to carry on. After several hours we had the job done and when the Germans came back and ordered us to load up their truck we got the picture. They gave us a kick in the behind and fired a gun over our heads. I wet my pants, yes, I sure did! We ran away, hearing them laugh. I ran so fast I set a world record, I swear!

The stress under which we lived all the time was enormous. A man could step out his front door and never be heard of again. Everything had broken down. The Germans had robbed the country of every piece of machinery available, and then destroyed the buildings. They stole all the streetcars from the cities and no one seemed to be working anymore. My father went to the east of the country to find some food for the family. We had no idea if we would ever see him again. Many people went east on their bicycles only to be stopped by the Germans on their return and have everything taken away, including their bicycles.

We had two elderly neighbours whom I often helped, as they had no food at all and were doing very poorly. One morning I realized that I had not heard from them for a day or so and went to their door. The door was unlocked and when I entered I found them both dead in bed. Maybe they helped each other die, I would never know. They just gave up. I was very sad, as I had liked them a lot. The bodies were carried away on a handcart. I knew there was a mass grave where they all went.

The situation became intolerable. The mortality rate from hunger in the first twenty weeks of 1945 was 167% higher than that in the same period of 1944. The 3000 pre-war daily calorie level had dropped to below 400. Walking down the street I would literally wonder how many people I would see drop dead between my home and my destination. Once an elderly man collapsed and fell against me. There was someone who had a steady route with his cart to just pick up the bodies of people who had died in the streets.

I was in the middle of all of that. It is no wonder that my nerves were shot. If I saw a German I hid straight away, because they were picking up ever-younger boys. Many so-called Germans were Russian prisoners in German uniforms who had to do their dirty work. At least they stayed alive, well, until Uncle Joe Stalin got his hands on them.

By the end of April I quit eating altogether. My stomach just could not accept the garbage that was left to eat. I chewed an old piece of leather just for the sensation of eating something, but I did not care anymore. Our neighbours on the other side, whom I did not know very well, also died. I prepared for the end.

An agreement was worked out with the Germans

whereby Allied planes could fly over the cities, parachuting large tins of dry, toast-like bread. Eating regular food would have killed people. Their stomachs and bowels just would not support it anymore.

Then, on May 5, 1945 the Canadians liberated us. People screamed, sang, and cried. They cried lots. But there was an aftermath for many, including me. Right after the liberation I went to work in an officers' hotel, where I became a waiter in a matter of hours. I got close to food, yes, real food. But then I got diphtheria. My last resistance vanished and the doctor had to get the life-saving serum from the Canadians. If this had happened just days earlier, I would not have survived.

For six months I was totally paralyzed. My mother had to spoon-feed me because I could not lift my arms. A nurse came every day to stick a long needle with vitamin B12 into my backside, and eventually I recovered.

This brings me to the end of my story. I can still hear the German boots marching on the road. I can still hear the soldiers singing that they will conquer England. I remain extremely sad about the people - many boys my own age - who did not survive. Even though 65 years have passed, my experiences of that time are very much with me. They still make me so sad!

The milk was sold out

Pauline Hofman

On a particularly wintry day in January of 1945, my mother told me to go and buy a bottle of milk from one of three dairy farmers with whom we were acquainted. Mamma handed me the bottle in a handbag and fifty cents. I really did not want to go as it looked so miserable outside. It was 4 p.m. and dusk had already set in. If the first farmer had no milk I was to go to the next one.

My long pants, made from an army blanket, kept me pretty warm but I had no mittens and my hands were freezing. I hung the handbag with the bottle in it around my neck and stuck my hands in my coat sleeves. With a shawl around my head and neck I looked like a rather old eleven-year-old. When I got to a checkpoint at a bridge the soldier guarding it looked the other way and I hurried as fast as my worn shoes allowed.

The first farmer, Ammerlaan, had sold all of his milk allowance. Ten minutes down the road was the farm of the Van Niekerks who were friends of my parents. I was sure they would sell me some milk, but I was out of luck and they were very sorry. Now I had to cross the frozen river to the third farmer, the Kortman family. Days earlier an icebreaker had broken up the ice in the middle of the river but the chunks of ice had frozen over again. While darkness set in I carefully chose my path and made it safely across. The farm looked deserted and dark and I was hesitant to knock. A young girl opened the door and asked if I had come for milk. I told her I had already tried two other farms. Here too, all the milk had been sold.

By now it was dark and I was getting very cold. Should I stay on this side of the river and cross closer to home? But that meant having to cross another bridge and it was a longer walk. I opted to go back the way I had come. Carefully, skipping over chunks of ice sticking out from the frozen river I found my way. Close to the other side I slipped and fell. All I could think of was that I was glad there was no milk in the bottle and that the bottle had not broken. I got up and hurried home. By now it was pitch dark. Electricity had been turned off and there were no lights anywhere. However, I found my way home.

My sisters had already come back, and the food from the soup kitchen was being kept warm. Mamma asked me about the milk and I handed her the empty bottle and the fifty cents. Her face became so sad. "Did you go to all three farmers?" she asked. I told her they were all sold out, and joined everyone at the table. It hurt me to look at my mother's sad face. The stew was made from potatoes and rutabagas with tulip bulbs instead of onions. We said our prayers and slurped up our portions... without milk.

The milk was often used to make butter and then the remaining liquid was made into breakfast porridge with barley and syrup made from sugar beets. We never liked it; it was always burned. The next morning we each got two slices of whole wheat bread with cheese, which to this day is still my favourite breakfast.

A birthday present

Pieter Koeleman

My friend's grandfather lived outside of our village. Opa used to stand in front of a table loaded with sugar beets, holding a peeled sugar beet against his chest and cutting off a big slice for each of us. I had no idea how that should taste, but it was something to eat, that was the main thing. When my younger sister had her birthday in March of 1944 there were not the usual gifts. For days mom was busy boiling sugar beets producing a whole bucket of pulp, but the birthday girl was happy with her present: a jar of sugar beet syrup. So were we!

We had to be thrifty. Nothing was thrown away. For a long time Mom managed to put some food on the table, but it was getting ever harder. Dad worked a shift in the soup kitchen. The men stood on a platform, stirring the stuff in the enormous kettles with a long stick. Close to noon you went there to fill a big pan and then go home to eat. It was usually a watery concoction of potatoes one day and cabbage the next. It never had an attractive smell. It was getting worse and towards the end we often had tulip bulb soup. This was an awful tasting and sickly smelling brew, but there was nothing else. One ate it under protest. One day people from Leiden, about seven miles east of us, came to the door asking if we had something to eat for them. They cleaned out whatever was left in our pan. To this day, if you were to put out twenty cups of soup and one was the tulip bulb brew I would be able to pick it out blindfolded.

Manna from heaven

Ralph Schotsman

I remember very well the Hunger Winter, and the women and children looking for food for their families. We lived in Harderwijk, close to the main highway from Amersfoort to Zwolle, and I often saw the trekkers. Sometimes the Germans took their food away from them when they reached the IJssel bridge. Men could not go for food because they risked being picked up by the Germans and sent to Germany to work.

My father was the manager of a factory called the Fino Fabriek, where they made soup, Maggi bouillon cubes, puddings and similar items. The Germans permitted the Red Cross to use part of the factory as a soup kitchen to feed those trekking for food. Since my father was the manager, my siblings and I got soup too, it was so good!

My parents took in many tired and hungry trekkers who just needed a place to rest or sleep. My mother told us one morning that some bed sheets had gone missing. She knew where they had gone but it did not upset her as our guests had obviously taken them to trade for food. Towards the end of the war many people in the cities had died; starvation took many of them. At that young age I learned a valuable life lesson: do not waste food because many people don't have any.

It must have been spring 1945, when I saw a wonderful thing in Harderwijk. Lancaster planes were dropping shiny tins on an open field near IJssel Lake. This time they were biscuits, not bombs. Those biscuits were manna from heaven. I will never forget that day.

I was sent to Noordlaren

Susan Rombeek

In The Hague that last winter, sugar beets became an important part of our diet. We sliced, cubed, and ground them to use in various recipes. Our street had one hand-cranked meat grinder, which was loaned out to whoever needed it for a sugar beet dish. We baked bread from tulip bulbs or fried them in oil. We got a very small loaf of grey bread, about three inches high and no more than twelve inches long. That was for a family of six people. My father would measure it and give us our allotment for that day. You could decide for yourself when you wanted to eat it, with no dinner planned. One day my little brother stole my piece, but that was understandable.

I often stood in line for hours at the soup kitchen. Sometimes fresh fish would be available, and I remember having to sit for hours outside the church on Pomona Square from where the fish was distributed. The other people waiting tried to cheer things up as much as possible.

We could not heat our house any more, and my brother Niek and I chopped asphalt sections from the streets, to burn as fuel. We all lived upstairs in one room with my grandmother.

Sometimes I was invited by acquaintances who could spare a meal, or my brother would get a meal from people at their house. My father became very ill with hunger oedema. My mother and grandfather would go on food trips. Once they were shot at and had to find cover. Another time, the Germans took all their food. Once a week Niek and I could get a meal from an interchurch committee that tried to supply food. This group arranged transports of children to the northern provinces. Niek was sent off to Overijssel where a poor but caring family took him in. Later on I also got on a transport. We had to go to Soestdijk Quay in The Hague where barges lay ready to take us across IJssel Lake. There was straw for us to lie on. I think there were about fifty kids on board. I was rather sad, and had told my mother I would eat grass if only I could stay home.

Two of my cousins, whom I had never met, were on board too. My father told me to stay with them so that he could find me after the war was over. If I got into trouble I was to go to a minister for help. So we sailed off in the dark, first to Hoorn and then across IJssel Lake in a terrible storm. Lots of the kids were seasick. I had fresh air and actually enjoyed it.

In Noordhorn, people came by and said which child they would take home, such as two 11-year-old boys, or one six-year-old girl. The rest of us were transported to the next town and the same scenario ensued until most of us were accommodated. I wanted to go to Noordlaren and, in the dark, carried on with my cousins. However, they got off and I was left alone. I asked the driver to take me to the minister, who placed me with the school principal where I stayed till the war was over. Late in June my father managed to find me, and drove me home on his motorcycle.

Diluted milk

George van Rijn

I was born in Amsterdam in 1938. My father was sent to Germany to work in the BMW factory making tanks. Somehow he obtained forged identity papers and traveled back to Holland. We had a secret code when our relatives visited: if it were not the special ring of the doorbell, Papa would hide in the attic.

I became very skinny and frail. The Red Cross arranged with the Germans for permission to let some of the children leave the city and go to the north of the country to live with farmers. I was sent to Groningen to live with a farm family. When I first arrived I could not keep any food down. They diluted the milk until my stomach could hold it down. I was there for about six months.

Robbed of his food

Truce Kuyper

I n my family with teenagers we were able to make several trips during that last horrendous winter. My sister, Ank, and I headed north once. We went by train to aunt Geertje in Hoorn. In the meantime my father, brother and two friends had biked all the way to Enkhuizen. They were on their way back and got as far as Hoorn when one of the wheels on their bike collapsed. One friend went back to Amsterdam with the wheel where another brother fixed it. Meanwhile Ank and I sat on top of the potatoes, onions and beets to keep thieves at bay while the other guys took a breather at aunt Geertje's house. She needed firewood so my brother went out to look for some. He came upon a wooden sign saying "Ordnung Kommandantur". He thought that would make good firewood so he started pulling it up. That proved to be difficult because it was cemented in the frozen ground. He had quite a struggle to get it out. Then he walked back with that sign through the town of Hoorn.

When we were on the ferry we saw a man with a handcart and a boy of maybe eight who was so tired he could not take another step. I helped him push his cart and when we finally reached his house I left. Later I heard that while they had gone inside, some creeps from his street had robbed him of most of his food. I was livid with myself. Had I stayed they would not have had a chance; I would have fought them tooth and nail.

Letting go of the fear

Tine Steen-Dekker

We rode on borrowed bicycles with solid tires from our home in Enkhuizen to the village of Hensbroek, North Holland, where my maternal grandparents lived. We needed food. The distance was about forty miles. Cor and Jannie, my parents, bundled my sister Nora and me up in many layers of clothing. Nora was maybe sixteen months old and I was five years older. We ate breakfast of bread with sugar beet syrup and a glass of the buttermilk that Mom had traded for her engraved silver wedding ring. Saddlebags on the bikes held clean diapers, spare clothing, and our remaining bread and buttermilk.

Noortje rode in a woven reed basket that Father had secured on Mom's luggage carrier and I straddled a pillow on Father's luggage carrier. I remember feeling excited at the prospect of going to be with our grandparents and with their neighbours and friends who loved us. I knew we would be safe, get delicious food, a warm room, and much comfort. There were hardly any Nazis around Hensbroek. At Zwaagdijk we stopped to eat our lunch under the trees. Mother sat on the ground and breastfed Noortje. Father hid the bicycles in the underbrush. He warmed my feet by rubbing them and putting them in his armpits.

We didn't linger. After we rode a long wide road past farmhouses, we turned right to the village of Wognum, under the overpass towards the village church, then right again. I had been made aware that being on the road could be dangerous for Father. He had a doctor's letter of exemption due to his frail health, but you never knew. Also, the Germans could take the bicycles.

So far we had not encountered a soul and I had begun to let go of my fears. Seeing the church gave me a good feeling. Perhaps my parents felt the same way; they certainly did not expect to come around that corner to see an army truck and two Nazi soldiers blocking their way. We knew this was a raid. I felt fear stiffening my whole body. There was no turning back.

Mother went up to the soldier who was blocking the way and handed him her ID papers, which he read and gave back to her. Now it was my father's turn. I felt ice cold. Father produced his papers and just as he reached out to hand them to the soldier, baby Noor whimpered plaintively, the sound muffled by the blanket that covered her. Everyone heard it. The soldier put his hand out to take Father's papers, and then abruptly waved my dad on and turned away. Father and Mother quickly got on their bikes and Noortje stopped crying at once. After a short while my parents stopped and embraced. Father stroked our heads, whispering a few words.

We arrived at my grandparents' home as it was getting dark. Opa and Father put the bicycles in the shed; Mother, Noor and I went into the lovely warm living room. There was a good fire. Opoe put buns on the heater to toast them. Mother cried with relief while feeding Noor. I was given a bun with butter and molasses while sitting in a rocking chair next to the heater warming my feet. After eating I began to rock and suck my thumb, feeling the fear slowly seeping away.

One of the good Germans

Wilhelmus (Bill) Bongers

Dad worked in the *Wehrmacht* barracks as a cook, baking bread. Dad always made too much so he could go home with the extras. He would always give the neighbours some too. Then the Wehrmacht command changed and Dad's services in the kitchen were no longer required. He was given another job, looking after the gardens. Dutch farmers were still growing vegetables and fruit, and at harvest time, German spotters visited the farms. The farmers were told "You have all these vegetables; everything will be confiscated." An armed sentry would be placed on that farm, and my Dad was ordered to round up half a dozen men to harvest the crop and take it to the barracks. On the return trip to the barracks, they would stop at our house and those of the other men, and by the time they got to the barracks, only one-quarter of the load would be left. The Germans were told that hungry people from Amsterdam had stolen the rest.

During the Hunger Winter, handcarts pushed by people from Amsterdam came through Hoorn every day. My father took pity on one family, a father with two sons, whose cart was heavily loaded with three bags of potatoes and a bag of wheat. They had been robbed before, so Dad told them to come to our place, and their cart would be safe in our backyard. Dad baked them each a couple of "hearth cookies" on top of our potbellied stove. Early in the morning they left before we were up. The following Sunday, when getting ready for church, we found that Dad's shoes were gone, as were Mom's and those of my older brothers. We never again had Amsterdam folks staying overnight at our house.

My brother Ap and I made friends with Heinrich, the new cook in the Wehrmacht barracks. He was one of the good Germans; he hated to be away from his farm, his family, and all his animals. He often gave us food. One day we saw a large truck backing up to the barracks kitchen, then leaving again. In the kitchen, Heinrich was cutting up half a pig carcass and said he had no time for us right then. Ap told him that he had just run into the Ortscommandant and that Heinrich was to go and see him. Heinrich took off across the yard and Ap and I took off with half of the head and a ham section of the pig. We wrapped our coats around the meat and ran home as fast as we could. When we saw Heinrich again two weeks later, he told us we were bad boys for stealing from him, and that if we wanted something, we should ask him.

One evening the doorbell rang close to curfew time. Dad opened the door and there was Heinrich, much larger than usual. He asked if he could come in. "Yes, of course", Dad said, "what do you want?" Heinrich opened his coat, under which were all kinds of goodies such as meat, canned goods, sugar, and butter. Heinrich told Dad to choose one item since there were more people he had to visit. Dad chose a piece of meat. Heinrich slipped away and Dad stood there dumbfounded, holding close to fifteen pounds of meat. Later we heard that the Gestapo had found out what Heinrich was doing and had done away with him.

The new girl

Wilma Johannesma

We lived in Amsterdam, where I was born. My parents struggled to keep us children alive, as there was almost no food left. The local churches had made arrangements for children to be taken in by volunteer families in the country. I was taken in a freight truck to stay with a family that was already taking care of my baby sister. It was almost dark when we reached the big country house and we couldn't find the door leading into the house. We opened one door and to our surprise it had a cow inside; the next door housed pigs, and another chickens. In desperation I jumped up and down in front of a high window through which I saw some light. Finally someone came to let me in, and my chaperone departed. Once inside I sat down and watched as the couple's thirteen children trickled into the room to stare at me, the new girl.

After the war, we all went our separate ways. In 1978 my father took my husband and me to visit the couple that had saved my life, and I expressed my deepest gratitude. I have kept in touch with one of the girls, who was around my age, and we have been sending letters, talking on the phone, and visiting for more than sixty years, from the age of seven until now, when we are both widowed. I am so grateful that we have each other as lifelong friends.

Contributors

Bill de Groot was born in Bussum, North Holland, where his family spent the war. He came to the USA in 1964, where he worked as a Mechanical Engineer. He and his wife, Lisette, have two daughters and one son. They live in Asheville, North Carolina.

Adriana Heim was born in 1927 in Rotterdam where she worked for C&A Brennickmeyer, first as a salesgirl and then as buyer. She came to the USA when she was 29. She settled in Massachusetts, then six months later moved to San Francisco, where she worked as an accountant in a hospital. Adriana now lives in Las Vegas, Nevada.

Afine Relk was born in Bergen, North Holland and was six when the war broke out. She married an American soldier and came to the USA in 1957. They had four children. Afine and John live in Nampa, Idaho, in potato country with a view of the Boise Mountains.

Ann Hendren was twelve years old and living in Utrecht when the war started. She now lives in Salem, Oregon.

Atie Lunshof Holmes lived in Utrecht during the war, while her parents were in the Dutch East Indies. She now makes her home in Claremont, California.

Arie de Keyzer was born in Rotterdam in 1929, and lived there until 1947. He spent two years in Indonesia as a marine, and still publishes their Marine veterans' magazine, Qua Patet Orbis. He and his wife emigrated to Canada in 1967, where Arie started a garage business in London, Ontario. They have two sons and four grandsons, and live in Kilworth, just outside London.

Audrey Hoeflok was born in The Hague in 1929. She came to Canada in 1957 with her husband and two children, and now lives in North Vancouver, British Columbia.

Bep Crawford-Haagedoorn was born in Amsterdam, and was twelve when the war broke out. She now lives in Kamloops, British Columbia.

Bertine Strengholt sent her story from Mississauga, Ontario.

Cornelius (Con) Zaat was born in Kwintsheul, South Holland, in 1933. During the early 1950s the Canadian forces were advertising in Dutch music magazines for musicians to help organize military bands across the country. Con's brother signed up first, and Con followed a year later, coming to Prince Edward Island in 1955. He played clarinet, bassoon, saxophone, and several other instruments. He later taught music in the schools and played in the Island's symphony orchestra. He continues to live in Montague, Prince Edward Island.

Dirk Hoogeveen was almost thirteen when The Netherlands was invaded by Germany. His mother, who was the postmaster of Bleiswijk, was a widow with seven children, of whom Dirk was the only boy. Dirk came to Canada with his wife in 1953 and settled in

Regina, where he worked for the Saskatchewan Power Corporation. He has written a monthly column for De Krant, the monthly newspaper for Canadians and Americans of Dutch origin, since 1980.

Doortje Shover lives in Newark, Delaware.

Ella Hoogwater was born in 1923 and was active in the wartime Resistance, for which she received a commemorative medal. She emigrated to Montreal, Canada, where she married a man from The Hague. She returned to Holland for about 18 years, where her four children went to school and Ella did office work. She then emigrated to British Columbia in 1991, and now lives in Langley, British Columbia, where she still volunteers in a Bibles for Missions store.

Else Bevelander was a teenager during the war, living in The Hague. She and her husband came to Canada in 1958, where they had three children and built up a good life. They live in Willowdale, Ontario,

Truus Leader married her first husband, an American, in Amsterdam and then moved to California in 1956. They had two children. After her first husband passed away she remarried and she has been together with her current husband for 32 years now. Truus has always been deeply grateful to the Allied soldiers who liberated The Netherlands. She became a member and president of the American Legion Auxiliary in Napoleon, Ohio, where she still lives.

Art Bos was born in Amsterdam, and was eighteen

when the war broke out. He came to Canada in 1952, working as an engineer. His wife is deceased, and he has one son and one daughter. Art lives in Surrey, British Columbia.

Icke (Freddi) Weston-Bousema was born in Haarlem and was four when the war started. She came to Canada in 1952 with her parents and two little brothers. She lived in Edmonton, Alberta for almost thirty years before moving to Victoria, British Columbia.

Frank VanderKley lived with his family in The Hague, and was six when the war began. He emigrated to Canada in 1953 to escape the military draft, and worked on a farm in Alberta. He later became a lawyer, and now lives in Trochu, Alberta.

George Hansman was twelve when the war began, and lived in Amsterdam. He came to Dauphin, Manitoba with his wife and two children in 1949 and worked as a mechanical engineer with CNR. He also lived in Ontario, Newfoundland and Québec, and then in Peru and Venezuela. He ended his career as manager of a paper mill. He now lives in Stevensville, Ontario.

Gertie Heinen was born in Bunschoten-Spakenburg. Gertie now lives in Picture Butte, Alberta.

Hidde Yedema was born in Witmarsum in 1935 but grew up in Makkum, another Frisian town. He and his wife, Nelly, came to Canada in March 1950, the trip being their honeymoon. Hidde found work on their second day in Calgary. He and Nelly had five children, who went to school in Cornwall, Ontario, where Hidde ran a bakery. Nelly died in 2000, and Hidde now lives in Laval, Québec with his second wife, Louise.

Riekje Brandsma grew up in Friesland, where her father owned a shipyard. She was the eldest of six children and celebrated her 21st birthday on an emigrant ship on the Atlantic in 1954. Most of the family returned to The Netherlands, but Riekje and one of her brothers stayed in Canada.

Jantina Smittenaar was born in The Hague and was eight yeas old when the war began. She came to the USA in 1955, where she spent a year in Florida before moving to Maryland, where she currently lives.

Janna de Klerk was born in 1930 in Nieuwer-Amstel, close to Schipbol Airport. She came to Canada on April 1, 1953, landing at Pier 21, Halifax, and took the train to Glenavon, Saskatchewan. She and her husband spent three years in Regina before moving to Calgary, Alberta. They have five sons, fourteen grandchildren, and twenty-three great-grandchildren.

Jacoba Bessey was living in Haarlem when the war began, one of four girls. She now lives in Regina, Saskatchewan.

Jenny Blad was born in the city of Groningen in 1937 as the oldest of six. She worked in a garment factory in Holland from the age of fourteen. She came to Canada in 1958 with her husband of six weeks, and three words of English. Jenny now lives in Westbank, British Columbia.

Johanna Van Breda-Csank lives in Arcadia, California.

Jerry Meents was nine years old when the Germans invaded Holland. Jerry's father was Jewish; his mother was not. The family lived in Amsterdam in the Transvaal neighbourhood, which had a large Jewish population. He fought in the Israeli War of Independence in 1948-49. In 1957 he came to the USA with his wife, seven-year-old son, and $1.25 in his pocket. He lives in Ogden, Utah.

John Eyking was born in Beverwijk in 1931. He came to Canada in 1953, and married his wife, Jeanne, two years later. They had two daughters and eight sons. They own Eyking Family Farms, a mixed farming operation in Millville, Cape Breton, Nova Scotia. John and Jeanne now have 31 grandchildren and four great-grandchildren. Both remain active with their farm and farm market.

John Keulen was born near Chicago in 1931 to Dutch immigrant parents. They returned to The Netherlands when John was two years old and settled in the Frisian village of Bakhuizen. They emigrated to the United States for a second time in 1948 when John was seventeen. John lives in Port Orange, Florida.

Karel Stuut was born in March 1932 and grew up in Haarlem.
He and his wife came to Canada by way of Montreal airport in 1957 (the government had paid for his flight and given him $50 pocket money). Karel worked in telecommunications. He and his wife had four children,

and now have seven grandchildren. They live in Dollard des Ormeaux, Québec.

Karl Vandegoede was born just outside the city of Utrecht in 1929. He and his wife, Janet, emigrated to British Columbia in 1958 with their two children. They now live in a seniors complex in Kamloops, British Columbia. Karl and Janet have twelve grandchildren and even more great-grandchildren.

Maria Neijmeijer grew up in Abcoude, near Amsterdam, and emigrated to Canada in 1958. She first settled in Saskatchewan but spent thirty years on Vancouver Island with her husband and four children. Maria and her husband retired to Saskatoon, Saskatchewan.

Kees Vermeer was almost ten years old when the Nazis invaded Holland. In 1954 he emigrated to Canada. With a PhD in Zoology from the University of Alberta, he became a research scientist for the Canadian Wildlife Service, studying bird populations, water pollution, and habitat destruction. Kees also worked in Chile and Suriname studying the effects of pollutants on birds. He lives in Sidney, British Columbia

Lisette de Groot was born in the Dutch East Indies. When she was three years old her mother died and she went to stay with an aunt and uncle in Rotterdam for two and a half years. Her father remarried, and the family was living in Voorschoten when the war started. Lisette and her husband emigrated to Jacksonville, Florida in 1964. They retired to Asheville, North Carolina.

Maria Blöte Rademaker sent in her contribution from Cobble Hill, British Columbia

Michael van der Boon was born and raised in Scheveningen. During the war his family was evacuated to the Bezuidenhout section of The Hague. He now lives in Hidden Valley Lake, California.

Robert Colyn was fourteen when the war began. He went to school in Haarlem, while his parents stayed in the Dutch East Indies. His parents were interned in Japanese camps and he did not see them from 1939 until after the war. Robert married his high school sweetheart in 1951 and emigrated to Brazil. After four years there he took a job in Akron, Ohio, where he lived until 1962. After four years in The Netherlands, managing a brick factory in Tricht, he moved to Salinas, California, where he lives today.

John van der Meer was born in Indonesia, but when he was one year old his family moved to Holland. He came to Canada with his wife, Johanna. They lived in Nanaimo, British Columbia until his death early in 2012.

Pauline Hofman was born in Amsterdam, but her family moved away from the city to be near relatives in a more rural area. She now lives in Geneva, Nevada.

Pieter Koeleman was born in Noordwijk aan Zee, Zuid Holland. He came to Canada with his wife, Beja, in 1984 to visit Pieter's brother on Quadra Island, British Columbia. The following year they emigrated to Campbell River, British Columbia, with four teenage children. One daughter went back to Holland. The other three live near their parents with their children.

Ralph Schotsman lived in Harderwijk and was eight when the war broke out. In 1951, as an eighteen-year-old, he came to Canada with his parents. Initially living on a rat infested farm in Uxbridge, Ontario, for six months, the family moved to Hamilton, Ontario. Ralph lives there in a house he moved into in 1960.

Susan Rombeek grew up in The Hague. She emigrated to Washington in 1967 with her husband, Edward, boarding the Rijndam on the day he was discharged from the Dutch Navy. Susan worked in a department store before returning to university to get her Master's degree in counseling psychology, and then worked as a school psychologist. She lives on Guemes Island, near Anacortes, Washington.

George van Rijn was born in Amsterdam, and was not yet two when the war started. He emigrated to the USA in 1959 with his parents, one brother and one sister, sponsored by a church in East Wenatchee, Washington State. He and his wife now live in Tualatin, Oregon.

Truce Kuyper was born in Landsmeer, North Holland and was twelve when the war began. In 1950 she and her new husband moved to Australia, but in 1956 they moved to the Buffalo area in the US, and then to Los Angeles in 1959. Truce now lives in Huntington Beach. She has two sons, four grandchildren, and one great-grandchild.

Tine Steen-Dekker lives in Edmonton, Alberta.

Wilhelmus (Bill) Bongers was born in 1933 in Hoorn, North Holland. He moved to Canada and was active with the Royal Canadian legion in Bathurst, New Brunswick. His war memories were recorded by the Comité 4045 Hoorn in Dutch, and for the Legion in English. Bill died in 2011.

Wilma Johannesma was born in Amsterdam in 1937. She worked in youth hostels in Belgium and Switzerland from the age of nineteen. In 1960 she came to Canada, where she felt at home instantly.

The Dutch in Wartime series

Book 1
Invasion

Edited by:
Tom Bijvoet

90 pages paperback
ISBN: 978-0-9868308-0-8

Book 2
Under Nazi Rule

Edited by:
Tom Bijvoet

88 pages paperback
ISBN: 978-0-9868308-3-9

Book 3
Witnessing the Holocaust

Edited by:
Tom Bijvoet

96 pages paperback
ISBN: 978-0-9868308-5-3

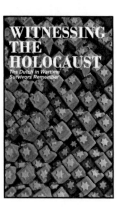

Book 4
Resisting Nazi Occupation

Edited by:
Anne van Arragon Hutten

108 pages paperback
ISBN: 978-0-9868308-4-6

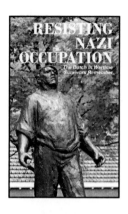

Book 5
Tell your children about us

Edited by:
Anne van Arragon Hutten

104 pages paperback
ISBN: 978-0-9868308-6-0

Book 6
War in the Indies

Edited by:
Anne van Arragon Hutten

96 pages paperback
ISBN: 978-0-9868308-7-7

Book 7
Caught in the crossfire

Edited by:
Anne van Arragon Hutten

104 pages paperback
ISBN: 978-0-9868308-8-4

Book 8
The Hunger Winter

Edited by:
Tom Bijvoet &
Anne van Arragon Hutten

110 pages paperback
ISBN: 978-0-9868308-9-1

Book 9
Liberation

Edited by:
Anne van Arragon Hutten

114 pages paperback
ISBN: 978-0-9919981-0-4

*Keep your series complete: order on-line
or contact Mokeham Publishing.*

CPSIA information can be obtained at www.ICGtesting.com
Printed in the USA
BVOW04s1018131014

370572BV00001B/30/P

9 780986 830891